LEARNING TO TEACH IN THE PRIMARY CLASSROOM

This text is specially designed to support student-teachers in the school-based element of their course. It provides accessible guidance, backed by numerous classroom examples, on the essential knowledge and skills needed to teach effectively. The chapters cover:

- Classroom organisation
- Planning for children's learning
- Teaching strategies
- Assessment, recording and reporting
- Self-appraisal

Each chapter contains essential information in concise and practical form. For students wishing to explore subjects in more depth, supplementary material at the end of each chapter includes analysis of curriculum and policy documents, case studies, suggestions for further reading and activities to try out in the classroom. Throughout, novice teachers are encouraged to think about how the basic skills fit together in their professional development and determine the sort of teacher that they will eventually be.

All four authors are experienced teachers who have taught in a wide range of schools and are now teaching at Edge Hill College, Lancashire, in the School of Teacher Education.

LEARNING TO
TEACH
—— IN THE ——
PRIMARY
CLASSROOM

Anne Proctor, Margaret Entwistle,
Brenda Judge and
Sandy McKenzie-Murdoch

RoutledgeFalmer
Taylor & Francis Group

LONDON AND NEW YORK

First published 1995 by Routledge
2 Park Square, Milton Park, Abingdon, Oxon, OX14 4RN

Simultaneously published in the USA and Canada
by Routledge
270 Madison Ave, New York, NY 10016

Reprinted 1995 (twice), 1997, 1999

Reprinted by RoutledgeFalmer 2001 (three times), 2002 (twice), 2003, 2005

RoutledgeFalmer is an imprint of the Taylor & Francis Group

© 1995 Anne Proctor, Margaret Entwhistle, Brenda Judge and Sandy
McKenzie-Murdoch

Typeset in Palatino by Solidus (Bristol) Limited
Printed in Great Britain by St Edmundsbury Press Limited, Bury St Edmunds

British Library Cataloguing in Publication Data
A catalogue record for this book is available from the British Library

Library of Congress Cataloguing in Publication Data
A catalogue record for this book is available from the Library of Congress

ISBN 0-415-11065-3

CONTENTS

FIGURES

DETAILED LESSON PLANS

NOTES ON AUTHORS

Anne Proctor is Principal Lecturer at Edge Hill College of Higher Education, with responsibility for the management of programmes for people preparing to teach in the Upper Primary age phase. Her particular interest is understanding the most effective ways of defining the roles of teachers and tutors in the professional preparation of student teachers. She recently completed a PhD in which she explored cooperation between teachers and tutors in the supervision of student teachers in school. The outcomes of the series of studies have been applied to the development of courses in teacher education/training and the development of mentor training programmes for teacher mentors.

Margaret Entwistle trained for secondary teaching and spent fifteen years in primary classrooms. She is now a tutor in the School of Teacher Education at Edge Hill College of Higher Education. Her present interests lie in exploring ways in which student teachers develop and learn and she has recently been involved with a Profile of Professional Development to help student teachers monitor their own professional development.

Brenda Judge has been headteacher of a large inner-city primary school for eight years and a primary teacher member of the Manchester Education Committee for three years. She is the initiator and co-author of *40,000 Minority* and *Primary Majority*, two booklets which prompted the establishment of primary headteacher groups across England and Wales and highlighted the inequalities of provision for primary-aged children.

Sandy McKenzie-Murdoch began her career as a primary school teacher where she became acutely aware of the challenge of meeting individual needs. This led her to pursue an interest in the psychology of learning and the study of teaching which has been the major focus of her career ever since. At present, she works with student-teachers and teachers both as a teacher trainer and as an educational psychologist.

1 INTRODUCTION

WHAT IS TEACHING?

A group of student-teachers had just completed the last week of their first term of a four year programme and they were reviewing their learning at that early stage. With the encouragement of their tutor and classteacher mentor they began to discuss and to identify personal strengths. They then moved on to think about 'where they wanted to be in four years' time' and 'how they would get there', anticipating their learning over the rest of the course. In other words they were thinking about the question 'what is teaching?' Below are some of their comments to each other.

'I don't know what it is that *you* do, Anna. It's quite magical. There they were, all fidgeting and restless and ready to be really naughty, and the next thing they were just as good as anything, all ready to listen and looking at you quietly.'

'Yes, and Richard, my teaching partner in the classroom, he is so really good at explaining things to the children, you could see that they were following and understood.'

'But isn't that because he listened to them properly in the first place? You know when we listened to that tape of him questioning the children about his sundial? We said that he made the children feel valued.'

'Yes but he'd planned it so carefully, too, hadn't he? But then he nearly spoiled it all with that dreadful writing on the blackboard!!'

As they talked they collected together their ideas under two main headings:

- what you needed to learn to do
- what you needed to learn to be

The lists that emerged show how these student teachers saw the two faces of teaching, the deliberate and learned skills or the more intuitive response to children and events. Here are some of the things which they listed under the two headings.

THE SKILLS OF TEACHING	THE QUALITIES OF A TEACHER
Teaching You need to speak clearly and use your voice properly with expression	
Questioning the children is more complicated than I'd thought – we need that skill	It's having a feel for the class, knowing how to get interest and involvement

Part of the skill of questioning is listening carefully to the children and understanding them

It's about being a good listener as well as telling them things

My lettering is awful, I'll have to learn to print properly

The children can tell if you care about what you are doing

Managing

You need to be able to organise groups

Teachers have to be leaders. The children have to see them as leaders. So do other teachers often too

We'll have to learn a lot more about discipline and how to deal with problems

You need to give off a sense of assurance

Classroom control, that's what I need to find out about

It's amazing what a difference it makes if you are able to speak with confidence, even if you don't feel it

Understanding children

I need to know more about children's special needs

It's all about getting the best out of children

You need to recognise and teach the different abilities in the class

The main thing is to make all the children feel valued

I'm going to find out about different faiths and cultures

You need to listen with understanding to parents

Planning

Teachers have to learn how to plan. They need to know about the National Curriculum

I can see that I'll have to be a lot better organised

The group decided that above all teachers would have to enjoy their work, care about children and their families and become really involved in their work.

In their informal discussion, that group identified some important characteristics of their chosen profession. Teaching involves:

- the learning of new skills
- the application of theoretical knowledge in a practical situation
- an enquiring and reflective approach to present practice and new situations
- a professional commitment to children and their parents as well as to teacher colleagues

PURPOSE OF THE BOOK

This book has been written as a guide to trainee teachers in the development of the initial skills and competences of teaching as well as the attitudes and expectations outlined above. It is also written for the teachers who will work with trainees in those early stages.

No book can hope to provide all the background which a beginning teacher will need and this book certainly does not attempt that awesome task. Instead the intention is to:

- provide a framework within which the different aspects may be placed so that the relationships between the parts may become apparent
- offer guidance in the development of some of the skills which teachers need to be able to put into practice
- indicate some of the issues/ideas which are presently preoccupying teachers, educational administrators and politicians

- offer help and encouragement in developing that reflective approach which is essential for professional development

FORMAT OF THE BOOK

The book is divided into five chapters: contexts for learning, planning for learning, teaching strategies, assessment, recording and reporting, and self-appraisal through profiling. The chapters are intended to cover basic teaching skills which a new teacher will require, in as clear and straightforward a way as possible. Each chapter will include examples which are intended to clarify the text and help the reader to link the information to the classroom context in which they are placed. Often the text will include techniques which the reader can use in the classroom situation.

All of this is intended to provide the trainee with practical help in planning for and implementing teaching and enhancing children's learning. However, as we have suggested above, teaching is more than the successful putting-into-practice of a number of simple techniques; it is the development and reflective adaptation of complex strategies to meet the personal and educational needs of children. In the early stages the trainee will be observing classroom practice and then with the help of colleagues trying to put into practice certain teaching strategies. As the trainee becomes more and more competent so s/he will be observing the children's learning and evaluating her/his own teaching. In evaluating the teaching, the trainee will refer to:

- feedback from the children
- discussion with teaching colleagues
- expectations of parents and carers
- documentation from the Department for Education
- appropriate literature on curriculum development and educational research

Each chapter has been planned with this process in mind. The main body of the chapter gives an outline of basic information which will provide you with a foundation for action. At the end of each chapter there are two further sections. *Section 1: Background* offers supplementary material, summarises a number of contemporary educational issues, and refers you to further sources of information and discussion. *Section 2: Activities* suggests a number of activities which you may use to extend and deepen your understanding of the material which has been introduced in the main body of the chapter.

We have already stressed the real importance of dialogue in developing understanding of teaching/learning and professional development and, in planning these activities we intend that they will be shared by the trainee and the mentor. In this way they will stimulate the professional discussion which will probably go far beyond the activities described.

Many of the examples in the chapters and the activities at the ends of the chapters are ones with which the writers are very familiar and which they have used successfully with student-teachers in the past.

CONTENT OF THE CHAPTERS

In choosing the content of the chapters our intention has been to follow the logical requirements of an intending teacher.

Chapter 2 looks at the context of the classroom in which a teacher will work with the children. There is a consideration of both physical factors which impinge upon planning and teaching in a positive or negative way, like space resources, attractiveness of the surroundings; and factors which need development in order to ensure good working conditions and a supportive environment for children's learning, like the organisation of the furniture, use of display area, management of materials, sympathetic use of personal space. Also important in this chapter is the nature of the interaction which is allowed to take place between the people (children and adults) in the classroom. This will depend upon the people themselves as well as upon the procedures which encourage their interaction. Children will learn better and feel secure in a well-ordered and supportive environment.

As has already been pointed out, the breadth and depth of the discussion is influenced by what it is possible to include in a basic text. It is not intended in the chapter, for example, to discuss the nature of child development or the social psychology of interpersonal relationships. However, the importance of these factors is indicated and reference made to other texts.

Chapter 3 explores the way planning for children's learning may be carried out. It begins with the details of lesson planning since that is where a trainee will begin. The first step is to understand the intentions which teachers have for children's learning and this leads on to a consideration of the best ways of achieving those objectives and assessing the outcomes of learning. Sound planning requires the teacher to have a good knowledge base; a clear understanding of the expectations embedded in the National Curriculum; a sensitive perception of the needs of individual children; and a sensible understanding of what can be achieved in a specific context. It is recognised that lesson planning develops from the long-term and medium-term planning which has already taken place in school and the ways in which schools and teachers may tackle this are explored.

Part of the planning process is a consideration of effective teaching strategies and these are explored in *Chapter 4*. There are many ways of encouraging learning and these need to be matched to what is to be learned and what the learner already knows or is able to do. This chapter identifies different teaching/learning strategies and attempts to show how decisions will be made about their implementation. Resources of various types enhance learning and the use of some of these is also considered.

Chapter 5 concentrates on the important and related areas of assessment of children's learning, recording and reporting. Teachers assess in order to identify children's achievements and difficulties and evaluate their own teaching. This information needs to be recorded in meaningful ways and then reported to those people who have an interest in it and a right to receive it. All of these aspects will receive consideration in Chapter 5, again with reference to other sources for further study.

As professional people, teachers are concerned with the development of their own expertise, and headteachers and governors are concerned about the continual development of the school staff as a whole. *Chapter 6* looks at some procedures for appraisal which teachers can use in a systematic way to scrutinise their own practice. Such an approach is a positive way of recognising strengths and identifying areas in which teachers may benefit from in-service provision as well as help from colleagues in school. A profile of professional competency is explored as well as procedures which teachers may adopt for personal appraisal.

AGE SPECIFICITY

The primary age phase extends from Reception children to Year 6 children, i.e. from age 5 years to age 11 years. Many primary schools also have Nursery classes for children age 3 and 4 years. The principles which inform teaching and learning are relevant across this wide range. However, the implementation of those principles will be different in different contexts. The text is intended to help your understanding of these important principles and the examples offered will, as far as possible, be pertinent to different situations. If necessary the age of the children will be identified, but at other times only the levels of the National Curriculum will be given. Sometimes your attention will be drawn directly to situations which may require different handling and the Bibliographies will lead to texts which will help you in applying principles of teaching and learning to meet the needs of individuals.

CURRICULUM EXAMPLES

In outlining approaches to teaching, learning and assessment the book makes use of examples of planning and teaching related to specific areas of the primary curriculum. Such a book cannot possibly outline all the curriculum content to which primary children should have access. It will be the responsibility of trainees and their mentors to ensure that the guidance offered in the text is related closely to knowledge and understanding of the primary curriculum.

USING THIS BOOK

Because people learn in different ways and because a book such as this has different functions for different people, it would not be helpful for us to outline a definitive way of using the text. However, it may be helpful to readers if we remind you of the way in which the text has been written and the implications that has for its use.

1 We have tried to show that this book offers only an outline or framework which will offer practical help and act as guide to further study and reflection.
2 We have also tried to indicate the interaction with other professionals which is necessary for reflection, re-appraisal and development. In other words the material in the book should be shared with others, i.e. a mentor, other teacher colleagues, other student-teacher colleagues.
3 Finally, we have tried to emphasise the problem-solving nature of teaching. Any action which a teacher (trainee or experienced) takes should not be taken just because somebody else says it should. A good teacher is able to explain and justify the procedures s/he uses and a trainee will want to start as s/he means to go on.

With these principles in mind the book has been written in such a way as to facilitate learning. The chapters are written in the order in which they are likely to be used and each offers practical help. We recommend that you read *Chapter 2* before starting on your school-based work. When you get into school it will be helpful to discuss some of the observation techniques with the class teacher to decide if it would be appropriate to use them. The outcomes of your observations will be much more useful to you if you are able to share them with other people and use them in more than one class.

Chapter 3 gives some quite specific advice about factors which need to be taken into account when planning a teaching session. These will seem very laborious to the practising teacher. However, it will be helpful to you to go through the whole process in the early stages in order to help you recognise the salient factors. The discussion of medium planning in this chapter may be left until you have a little more experience.

You will certainly want to give quite close attention to *Chapter 4*, on teaching strategies, in the early stages. A cursory reading will give you some ideas of the content, but as you undertake more and more practice you will want to keep returning to the appropriate sections in the chapter in order to refine and develop your teaching. With increasing experience, the strategies will make more and more sense to you and encourage the reflective process.

From the beginning, assessment will be an integral part of the planning of your teaching sessions. As you begin to know children better, however, and also to develop confidence you will find greater opportunity for the close observation which assessment requires. This will be the time to tackle *Chapter 5*. Take the opportunity to identify the different modes you are using, to consider better ways of getting evidence and recording it, the criteria you are using to make judgements and most importantly the impact that the assessment of children is having on your teaching.

All the time you will be judging in some way your own teaching performance. This may be in discussion with your mentor or colleagues, or it may be as a result of the feedback which you are receiving from the children. However, there will come a time when you will want to formalise that evaluation and that is the time to tackle *Chapter 6* on appraisal. The procedures which are recommended in this chapter will help you to approach appraisal in a systematic and positive way. The elements of the profile will give you the language to use in discussing planning, teaching and children's learning. Perhaps most importantly it will offer an opportunity to record your achievements. As you do this you will want to return to specific chapters in order to move on, especially to the sections 1 and 2 at the end of each chapter.

The use of sections 1 and 2 will depend very much on the nature of the training programme which you are undertaking. The aspects considered are likely to be part of your training programme and it will be helpful for you to consider them when they arise as part of your taught course. If you wish to tackle these sections in your own time, then we recommend that you stagger their use to match as far as possible aspects of your teaching. Talk about a plan of action with your mentor and organise the activities and the supporting discussions which will be necessary in such a way that you allow yourself time to think about the outcomes of the activities and the supporting reading. Try to see them as small units of study related to your work in the classroom.

It only remains to say 'good luck' and 'enjoy your teaching'!

2 THE CONTEXTS FOR LEARNING

In this chapter you will:

• be introduced to the significance of context as an influence on children's learning and social development and on teachers' intended and actual effectiveness;

• identify aspects of:
  - children's intellectual and social functioning,
  - classroom layout and arrangements,
  - the general 'fabric' of classroom life,
which influence the success of classroom enterprises at individual and group levels;

• be encouraged to apply such knowledge to actual classroom situations so as to influence learning outcomes in a positive direction.

THINKING ABOUT CONTEXTS

Imagine that you are standing at the door of the classroom which is to be 'yours' for the next few weeks of School Experience. It is still quite early and the children have yet to arrive. 'Your' classteacher is busy in another part of the school and has told you to make yourself at home. The space you are now surveying is going to be very important to you as it will be the physical setting for your teaching experience, so take a little time now to speculate on all the objects, events and social relationships within this classroom which will affect the success of your forthcoming teaching experience.

Make a list of the things you think of now and you will be able to compare it with the ideas which you will meet in this chapter. In your imagination you have been thinking about the various contexts which affect learning.

The classroom *in use* is a highly complex and fascinating system. To use a little of the language of systems theory, the classroom, as a setting where learning takes place, is made up of many *elements* – for instance, the physical context can be very important in influencing how well children and teachers accomplish what they set out to do. Other elements within the classroom system include aspects of social interaction between children and teacher and amongst children, they include aspects of the curriculum being presented to children and the teaching/learning approaches which have been selected as most appropriate. Such elements make up what we mean by the 'contexts for learning'. They are important in influencing the quality of learning outcomes and the sense of satisfaction felt by the partners in the classroom system – the children and the adults who work in the classroom together.

In this chapter we shall be 'unpacking' this idea of contexts for learning. We will look at a range of characteristics in people and at factors in environments which have been found to have an effect on the quality of learning outcomes. To return to the idea of elements within the classroom system, the main elements we shall be considering fall into the following groups:

- physical context, e.g. space, facilities, layout
- psychological context, e.g. individual differences in how children learn
- social context, e.g. friendships

It's very important at this stage to emphasise that these elements which influence learning outcomes, though listed separately, also interact, so that for instance an aspect of what is to be taught/learned may be more successfully presented to children working in small groups with friends in a particular kind of classroom layout. It is for this reason that we began this chapter with the description of the classroom as highly complex!

When we have finished unpacking this very full parcel of ideas labelled contexts for learning, you will be able to consider physical and non-physical influences on learning with a much more critical eye *and* will be able to think about organising them so as to maximise the chance of good quality learning outcomes being achieved. You will also be able to see how your consideration of contexts forms a part of the whole planning package described in Chapter 3 *and* how contexts have a bearing on teaching, which is the focus of Chapter 4.

If you are wondering at this stage if such aspects of contexts as we've listed are really important in influencing human behaviour – of which learning is one type, of course – just consider these points.

- Researchers found that it was possible to make predictions of how much children would take part in class activities just by considering the seating arrangements in the classroom.

- When *you* are being a learner, don't you like to choose where to sit – in the library or lecture room – and to choose how much noise to have in the backgound and to decide whether to work early or late, in short bursts or in long spells? Should we expect our pupils to be very different?

- It's quite clear that architects and interior designers know how much contexts – physical, psychological and social – influence human behaviour, since they go to great lengths in choosing particular characteristics of context in their attempts to get us to stop and look or to move quickly through a space, to buy or to eat and so on.

Let's begin our examination of contexts by thinking about the 'physical context' as this is probably the element which would strike you first as you looked in through your imaginary classroom door.

THE PHYSICAL CONTEXT

The physical appearance of the classroom is probably the most obvious element in the system which you identified when you made the list suggested at the beginning of this chapter. This is not surprising, since the idea of the setting having an effect on events and outcomes is very familiar.

As you consider the range of ideas which will be presented in the next few pages, it will help you if you think of an actual classroom which you know quite well; it will be ideal if you are currently working in a classroom which you can use as a 'test-pad' for this range of ideas and Activity 1 in Section 2, pp. 34–5, of this chapter will help you to focus your thinking.

By the time you have completed this part of the chapter you will be better able to understand how the arrangement of the physical setting can aid you in achieving your intentions for children's learning. From this understanding you will be able to work out what changes you may want to make to a particular setting prior to a teaching session. Your aim will be to produce a better chance of successful outcomes with the minimum of disruption and without causing offence to others who may also be working in the space at other times.

In most schools the classroom arrangements are generally quite unchanging in terms of the layout of furniture, the location of storage facilities and the purposes to which space is put. There may be good reasons for this – not least that frequent and unnecessary changes can be tiring, time-consuming and irritating – but we must grasp useful opportunities to support children in their learning by active and regular thought at the planning stage about ways in which the physical context should be arranged. In fact, changes in the physical characteristics of the learning environment are often found to be interesting to the participants and pedagogically worthwhile, so it is important for teachers to keep some flexibility in how they plan and use the space and other facilities available to them.

(Try Activity 1 in Section 2, pp. 34–5, now.)

After completing Activity 1 you will have brought a lot of specific information to mind and you are in a good position to consider the following points and questions, which are intended to act as further triggers to your thinking. Use the situations which you have visualised to 'personalise' the ideas you will meet. The main focus here is to think about how the teacher must actively consider the physical context and its various effects on the learning which is being planned for and thus whether changes will be needed and of what type.

There are numerous types of classroom settings to be seen in schools; you will already be familiar with many as both pupil and beginning teacher – arrangements such as open plan, semi-open plan, and closed. Within these types children can be seated in small groups (four to six), in bigger groups (up to ten), in pairs arranged in rows, or occasionally singly. Section 1 contains some diagrams of layout for you to consider.

In many cases the most dominant factor in determining the use of space will have been the furniture rather than the teacher's active consideration of space as an aspect of the classroom system which can have a powerful effect on the outcome of learning opportunities. Obviously, the furniture will be a significant element in the system but it must not become more influential than the need to make the system serve the learning. So, as you think about the following points, try to avoid being put off by purely concrete objections such as 'the desks in my classroom would be too heavy for that', or 'the school I'm in doesn't use files to store children's work', at least until you've given thought to the principle which the point or question encapsulates. For convenience the next part of the chapter will consider layout, movement, access to information and equipment and comfort as separate aspects of the physical context although, of course, in reality these aspects operate together and sometimes affect one another.

Layout of the classroom

Using the space well

The way in which furniture and facilities are arranged within a space can send clear signals about what is to happen in the space. You know from your own experience that if you walk into a room where all the chairs are arranged in a circle, the likely activity will be different from that in a room where all the chairs face the front. You will also probably have had the experience of actually rearranging the furniture to accommodate a different kind of activity. This principle of 'signalled activity' is important when we think about classroom layout, for it shows us that since the arrangement of the furniture leads to expectations about the kind of activity to take place, we must ensure that the layout and the activities we plan to happen do not conflict. A common example of conflict occurs when children sit in a highly sociable group arrangement where they share space with others next and opposite to them and yet are expected to sustain periods of individual effort with negligible interaction. In fact the children pay more attention to the social seating pattern than they do to the task and the teacher will find themselves having to remind children about the 'rules' for quiet, individual work on a fairly frequent basis, often with an increasing sense of frustration. Such conflicting messages can be reduced when teachers give thought to seating patterns. Even something as relatively quick as preparing for the quiet, individual work session by moving chairs and tables so that children do not immediately face one another, will have a noticeable effect on noise levels, time on task and quality of outcome, once children have got used to the procedure. Similar simple manoeuvres can be tried so that children who need to concentrate are not distracted by others who need to move and/ or make noise. Again, some children will need to keep work clean and will be disturbed if they have to work near children working on messy activities. A further example of avoiding potential conflict is to arrange for the greatest physical separation of space where children are engaged in necessary routine tasks while others are working on highly exciting activities.

You may think that simply rearranging the layout will not produce any great effect on learning outcome and you would be partially correct in this. The teacher must also ensure that children know what to do and know what others will be doing, for instance by the way in which the session is begun with a review of everybody's activity before groups and individuals settle to their particular work. When children know what is expected *and* the environment supports this, they will soon get on with their own work and there will be a minimum of the non-task related behaviour which can waste so much learning time.

Organising the workspace

Has it struck you that you can work out quite a lot about children's status in the class by observing where the teacher asks them, or puts them, to work? 'Good' children often sit around the fringes of the room, 'naughty' children are kept near the teacher's main workplace (even if the teacher doesn't actually spend much time there) or banished to the very edge to work with their back to the main arena of action. Teachers may have very good reasons for these decisions in which case they can be justified, but there are times when the situation just evolves through unplanned decisions and the signals being given by location and expectation are in conflict. We can illustrate this by two simple examples. If the compliant children are seated near the back and the sides of the room they may begin to feel somewhat out of the main action and may not continue to be so compliant − not what the teacher intends at all! If the child who spends too much time off task is placed where the teacher can 'keep an eye' on them, that may involve putting the child in one of the most distracting locations in the room − where people go to leave completed work, to pick up equipment, to wait for the teacher and so on. Again, not what the teacher really intended. So, the key to avoiding conflict between layout and teacher expectations of learning outcome is to begin with clear intentions and then to actively consider how the arrangement of the room will best support these plans.

Not only must we pay attention to children's workspaces but also to our own as teachers and to those of any other adults who may also work in the classroom. It is common for teachers to have little dedicated space of their own as they find it more efficient and pleasant to move around amongst the children while they are working; however, even in these circumstances there will need to be somewhere which acts as storage point for records, supply point for some equipment, reception point for completed work and so on. Teachers' desks or tables are often arranged so that the teacher can sit behind them and survey the class when many teachers spend very little time making such use of the space. When space is at a premium, as it often is in classrooms, it makes sense to place the teacher's workspace against a wall or cupboard back so that more use can be made of the space on the three remaining sides. Note, though, that this arrangement will have implications for subsequent use of the workspace if the teacher is not to work with their back to the class; thus only certain short-term activities can take place there while the children are present. For longer activities the teacher will use space in a variety of places around the room. This example further illustrates that *planned* use of space in terms of activities and expected outcomes is an important part of the whole classroom enterprise.

Individual space/shared space

It is interesting to think about the merits of each child having a relatively permanent workspace of their own and set this against the idea of workspaces being tailored to particular activities and children moving around amongst them. The latter arrangement is commonly seen in classrooms for younger pupils; but seating patterns often become less flexible as the age of the pupils increases, although it is very common for classrooms to have at least a 'dedicated' wet area with tiled floor and sink, etc. Again, there will be no single right way to set out the classroom, the important point being that the arrangement must suit what is to go on in terms of learning. If each child always has their own workplace, space will be underutilised at times because the child will be working elsewhere, e.g. measuring the playground, but the advantages are that all will know where each should be at fixed points and each child has some feeling of security about 'their' space and place for belongings. If a system is used where space is 'dedicated' to particular activities and children work in different places at different times of the day, then arrangements have to be made for children to have ready access to their personal store of paperwork and equipment. One of the traffic jam situations referred to earlier often arises when numbers of children need to get at storage trays or shelves at the same time. This can be easily avoided, however, by forward planning on the part of the teacher and as children develop familiarity with efficient routines for moving about and accessing equipment.

At this point it will be useful for you to pause and review some of these ideas in terms of the plans which you drew of your 'test pad' classroom in Activity 1. Experiment with the idea of different layouts for different kinds of situation so that the arrangement of furniture and the use of space is most appropriate to the intended learning opportunities and outcomes. As you do this be sure to bear in mind that children must have clear sight of whatever they are asked to pay attention to, be it the teacher, the board, a wall or table display. It is not acceptable for children to have to spend much, if any, time twisted around in their seats, so think about moving the children and/or the object of their attention. Remember too, that it is unpleasant for any child, and even painful for some children with visual disability, to have to look at something against the light, so don't locate your teaching position in front of windows in your visualised new layout.

Finally, as you experiment, think about lines of sight – yours for all the children for most of the time and theirs for you. It's quite a useful strategy to think about the child's eye view of the classroom when you consider lines of sight. You could even try sitting at the child's level next time you are in the classroom for real. If children need to be able to see and be seen then the physical arrangement of the room must facilitate this.

Space for display

The last physical feature we shall consider in this analysis of the impact of layout on the learning environment concerns the arrangements made for display in the classroom. Here, we need to think about vertical and horizontal displays which might be observed or might be actively used by children. The purposes for which the displays are put up will largely determine the most appropriate location within the classroom layout. If close examination is intended then the materials must be easy to see – not too high or far away and in good light. If the display is one that children will want to spend time at, then it should not be in a high-traffic area but rather in a position where children will be undisturbed as they study the display or handle the artefacts and so on. If the materials on display are fragile or unstable, for example breakable items on loan or pictures made with chalks or pastels which will rub off, then, again, high traffic areas should be avoided. It is also useful to bear in mind that displays in some areas can become unattractive quite quickly as the effects of sunlight, water splashes and fiddling little fingers take their toll!

Look back at your plan drawings, paying particular attention to the space available for displays and consider how you could make best use of such space. Think too, of how you might arrange for extra display space or space for special purposes, e.g. for a large combined vertical and horizontal display within the total classroom space, and don't forget the child's eye view!

As you have been trying out various classroom layouts in your imagination you may have thought that they would involve a lot of furniture shifting which would be time-consuming and disruptive. This could happen, but not if the rearrangements are carefully planned. Simple moves can be accomplished quickly because the children know what to do and how to do it – these could be used on a regular basis, for example, all the children moving to the carpeted area for registration, class discussion or story and then to individual or group workspaces afterwards. More complex moves – say clearing floor space for some drama work – could be done with a group of children over a break or with all the children in a phased operation which the teacher has given them a chance to learn before expecting it to be done quickly and quietly. When the children know what to do and want to get started on the activity there will be much less chance of time-wasting and frustration.

Movement around the classroom

At certain times, movement is a very prominent feature of most primary school classrooms and giving thought to its management ahead of time can really pay dividends. Movement can be task-related, for example going to the bookshelf to check a fact; it can be routine-related, for example lining up before going out to play; it can be idiosyncratic, for example going to look at somebody's work out of curiosity.

You will already have begun to think about movement management as you considered the layout of the classroom – making sure that there was sufficient room for children to get at equipment safely and simply, looking out for traffic jams in routine movement patterns and so on, so we need not go into great detail about task-related and routine-related movement, but the notion of idiosyncratic movement may be new to you. As teachers, we are often concerned to limit idiosyncratic movement especially as children get older, probably because we tend to see such movement as allied to off-task behaviour. It is important to be able to distinguish whether the child really is off task or whether we have failed to predict that the child would want or need to move from their workspace at some point. An example of this lack of analysis would be when the teacher plans an activity which requires certain pieces of equipment to be used at certain stages whilst failing to arrange that each child actually has the equipment to hand when they need it. In this case the child is not deciding to move on a whim, which is what idiosyncratic movement involves, but is actually provoked to move by some aspect of the teacher's (incomplete) planning. Thus, whichever of the three types of movement we are considering, the need for careful forward planning is clear. It is also important to bear in mind that all human beings need a certain amount of movement and that youngsters are more active in general terms than adults, some youngsters being very active indeed. Thus, if you know that children in your class have difficulty keeping still and in one place for very long, you will need to adopt the two-fold planning approach of giving them opportunities to move legitimately and then helping them to gradually extend the length of time for which they can stay still encouraged by their experience of success at interesting tasks.

Whilst we are focusing on the management of movement we can also give thought to the specific needs of children for whom mobility around the classroom may be a challenge, as in the case of a child in a wheelchair or with leg-braces or poor gross motor control. In such situations forward planning is again important so that gangways are left clear, materials are stored at appropriate levels and carrying boxes or baskets are provided for small items which could otherwise be difficult for the child to carry. Once again we see how consideration of movement and consideration of layout are linked and it will soon become clear that the other aspects of access and comfort are also involved.

Access to information and equipment

If you were to shadow for a day a child in the class you have been thinking about and simply list all the ways in which they needed to be able to gain access to different kinds of information, it would surely be a very long list. For example, you might note that children need:

• to see board work or displays
• to consult books
• to listen to another child or an adult
• to converse with others
• to get at and use different types of equipment

(Incidentally, you would also be listing their task-related and routine-related movement, showing again how the aspects of the physical context which we are considering are linked together.) You would not be able to carry out such a shadowing exercise very often as it is so time-consuming, but it is well worthwhile thinking through in some detail in advance of the learning session exactly what children will need to be able to look at, touch, study closely, use, etc. so that you can be sure that you make the necessary arrangements for such activities to take place. For example, suppose you want a group of children to look at a picture and discuss it before producing a picture of their own. It is obvious that every child must have adequate sight of the picture for a sufficient period of time. Without this, children will be less well prepared than you intended and will probably demonstrate their feelings of grievance at not being able to see. In such a case your forward planning must include conscious consideration of how you will arrange access to the information for each child; this will mean, for instance, thinking about the size and clarity of the picture to be discussed, the number of children who can see it well at one time, the location of the group for this and the next phase when they will do their own picture, whether you will hold the picture up or pass it round (bearing in mind what these pupils are used to doing in such circumstances), and so on. From this analysis you will see that the seemingly simple technique of showing something to children is in reality a complex situation which the teacher must think through carefully if it is to lead to the intended outcomes. Of course, as you become more practised in classroom techniques, the thinking-through phase of planning can be less elaborate but it should not become less conscious. The underlying fact is clear – if children are to acquire and use information effectively, as we intend, then they must have adequate access to it.

The same is true of access to equipment and facilities and a key element here is the physical organisation of such items. Remember the child's eye view. As you think through what you intend children to do and to use, ask yourself whether they can easily get what they need. Do they know where it is? Can they reach it safely or must you get it for them? If you really did make the list suggested earlier you would probably be surprised at the range of information sources, equipment and facilities which children make use of in a day. Some will be for their exclusive use, some will be shared with others though used quite frequently (erasers might come in this category in some classrooms), and some will be shared and used only occasionally.

Each of these categories requires a different kind of access which must be identified by the teacher and organised in advance. Simple and clear storage techniques are of great assistance in supporting access to information, equipment and facilities – techniques such as clearly labelled bookshelves, drawers, files and boxes which children can locate quickly and reach safely so that adults in the room do not need to break their own activities to find, fetch or reach materials. Careful thought given to organisation and maintenance (including tidiness) in advance will leave more of a teacher's attention and energy for the most important task of promoting and supporting children at the point of learning.

When you go into a classroom for a period of School Experience, you will mostly latch on to the procedures of storage and access already in place and which the children will be used to following. You may well feel apprehensive about making changes and, initially, you would be wise to take a little time to see how the procedures work in practice before trying to introduce variations; however, you may well find that discussion with your classteacher about your specific intentions will lead to some ideas for changes which affect children's access to information and equipment and then these elements must also be included in the planning. A simple example of this would be when you decide that it would be best to group children in a particular way and to have certain groups working in particular places in the room. In this case it is essential to think about each child's access to their personal equipment – pencil, ruler, word-book, reading book, etc. – so that there need be little disruption when children collect what they need in order to begin work. Teachers who move the children without their tidy boxes or trays quickly see the impact on movement patterns, traffic jams and general loss of calm in the room! So, as you think about *what* children will be doing and *where*, in terms of your lesson planning, you will also be thinking about layout, movement and access.

Comfort

You may think that this is rather a strange heading because no teacher would consciously arrange the physical environment so that children were uncomfortable. The aspects of comfort which will be described here are ones which are fairly concealed in the classroom and therefore easy to overlook. Think about the classroom you know as your 'test-pad' as you read down this list.

- Children need appropriate space in which to work, which means that they can lay out their materials so that they don't impede one another. For example, watch out for the *faux pas* of asking children to work on larger sheets of paper than their workspace will accommodate so that they overlap with one another – it causes irritation and disputes.

- They need space which is suited to their size. Children can vary greatly in size in a particular age group and some may need furniture of the 'next size up' if they are to be comfortable and produce the best quality work.

- A number of children have specific needs which will have implications for the kind of physical context they need. Here we can think of children with identified Special Educational Needs who require particular facilities in terms of lighting, assistance in hearing, room to move a wheelchair or stretch a braced limb, special tables which allow them to get close to their work from a special chair and so on.

Discussion with the classteacher will be crucial in providing the information and ideas which you will need in meeting such needs when you plan for and teach the children yourself. You will also find a number of useful books which will give you general information, some of which are listed in the Bibliography, p. 38.

The crucial role of careful forward planning is as clear in this aspect of comfort as it is in the other aspects we have considered under the general heading of physical context. At the beginning of this chapter we set out to consider how elements in the contexts for learning affect the quality of learning outcomes and what action the teacher can and should take to create the most supportive classroom system. It should now be quite obvious that the physical context is an element within the system which teachers are wise to pay plenty of attention to as they seek to create a classroom setting which best supports high-quality learning.

THE PSYCHOLOGICAL CONTEXT

When you made your imaginary survey from the classroom door at the beginning of this chapter, one of the elements you would have given early consideration to would be the effect of individual differences in children. We've already seen how, for instance, the variation in children's sizes in a group has to be taken into account in the physical context, now we will give some thought to a large group of individual differences which come under the heading of psychological context.

Whatever the extent of the experience you have already had in working with children in classrooms, you will know that they can show very different approaches to learning. Some children will work very slowly and carefully and be concerned to be correct before they commit themselves; other children will dash at the work, hardly giving themselves time to think at all. In another way you may have noticed that children seem to differ in terms of the amount of information about the task they like to get before they start on it. Some need a lot of detail about the steps involved; others seem content to get a general picture plus the starting point and then they will set off to work.

Such differences between children are important in the sense that they *do* have an effect on the learning progress of the individual and therefore the teacher must include them in consideration of contexts for learning when planning content and delivery.

Of course you will be well aware of the way in which individual differences in age and ability have a bearing on children's progress and we shall look briefly at those elements later in this section. At this stage we will concentrate on a range of tendencies which are *not* the same as differences in ability though they can have quite an effect on how well children do when they set out to tackle learning tasks. These are differences in the ways in which children tend to feel most 'comfortable' in learning. They have been given various names by various authors and researchers – learning styles, cognitive styles, learning preferences – but whatever we call them their impact is important and we need to take it into account when trying to arrange the best contexts in which learning can take place.

Differences in learning style

Perhaps you can bring to mind a classroom session which you have observed or taken charge of, where children were being asked questions as a preparation for some new work. You will have noticed how some children shoot their hands up before the question has been completed – and these will not necessarily be the most able children – whereas others (who may well have an answer) may have to be asked by name and then take quite a time to put their answer together. In this situation we are seeing differences in what has been called 'cognitive tempo' – a sort of 'speed of intellectual tickover'. It's important not to see the eager child (called 'impulsive' in this theory) as inevitably a bright child nor the less eager child (called 'reflective') as inevitably a less able child. In fact it may work the other way around in practice! In many learning situations *time* is required for the learner to put together their understanding of the task and the impulsive approach is unhelpful; in this sense the reflective approach is the one to encourage in *all* children whatever their individual tendency.

So how does the teacher make an impact on such a tendency? Go back to your recollection of the question session. Was there in fact a feeling that quick answers were what the teacher wanted? This might have been signalled by an urgent tone of voice, by rapid teacher response to impulsive answers, by a tendency to 'move on' if a child did not appear to know an answer straight away or if they gave an answer that seemed to go round the subject. Now, there are times when we want to encourage children to retrieve what they know quickly and efficiently and to work at an automatic level – for instance in recalling number facts or object names – and so a sense of urgency is a good signal to use. Equally there are many times when it is very important to signal to children that they will need to take time in order to have the best chance of a successful outcome because the type of complex learning which is often involved in school *does* take time. In these circumstances the teacher must plan and deliver material in ways which will help children to work well whatever their underlying tendency or preference. Sometimes this can be a very direct form of help such as saying 'I don't want you to answer straight away, give yourself time to think before you put your hand up'. At other times, the best approach may be to include in the teaching approach a gradual build-up of ideas and understanding through, for example, a technique like cascade discussion where two children discuss the topic then share their ideas with two more and refine their thinking as they go. The quartet only 'go public' to the whole group or class when they've had time to listen, think, compare and reflect in terms of the ideas of others.

In general terms, we can observe that children become less impulsive as they progress through the primary school and that the tendency to be impulsive at any age can be modified by reflective approaches in adults as models and by opportunities (such as the examples above) to practise working in reflective ways.

If we return to your experience of observing children as they tackle learning tasks, you may well have observed another way in which children differ in their preferred learning style. Some children like to have the task given to them as a series of steps which they then like to check as they go, without being overly concerned about the final outcome until they get there; others are keen to know about the end point when they are still at the beginning. Of course, the child who asks for step-by-step support *may* be showing their need for reassurance or their poor ability to retain a sequence of instructions in their head, but some children will be showing a real preference for encountering material and opportunities as a series of steps which they can work at in an organised way. The teacher's presentation will need to be quite different for these children than for those who are happy to be given the overall shape of the learning task and then set out on it.

How can the teacher manage to work with these contrasting underlying learning preferences, especially since there will be circumstances when the teacher will not know the children well enough to predict how individuals prefer to encounter tasks? The teacher's strategy in such a case is quite straightforward – it is to include both aspects in their presentation of the task. In other words to present the task both in terms of the overall goal and to spell out the steps to the goal which children will need to go through if they are to have the best chance of success.

There will be some situations when you will want all children to work carefully through step-by-step – as in a technology activity for instance – or, by contrast, to take the task as a whole – as in producing some highly 'atmospheric' poetry – and then the teacher's approach must include very careful and clear planning of what is needed. This then will be clearly signalled to the children and they must be supported in working in ways which may not actually be how they feel most comfortable.

We've looked at two varieties of learning style here – speed of intellectual tickover and the preference for different types of information about the task at the outset. There are several other types of learning style which have also been found to make a difference to the success of children's learning. There is a reference which you can use (Fontana, 1987) to read more about this subject. In thinking about all types of learning style a number of points are important for the teacher. First, these differences are real and do have an impact on the individual child's progress. Second, they are not the same as differences in ability though they can appear to produce similar kinds of effects in terms of relative success or failure. The third point follows directly from the other two – the teacher needs to pay close attention to such individual learning preferences because sometimes the style of the child and the demands of the task may not be entirely parallel and then the child must be helped to adapt and/or the teacher must work out ways of making the gap as insignificant as possible. The key to successful teacher action is the one you will meet time and again in this book – clarity about what it is you want to achieve and clarity about how you intend to achieve it.

Laying sound foundations for learning

You know yourself when you are embarking on new work, especially if you feel that it may be challenging (and most learners actually like a degree of challenge), that it helps you greatly if you have a reasonably clear idea of what it is you should be doing, at least in outline terms. It helps us to know where we are going in the task or group of tasks even if the nature of the task itself is quite open-ended and individually creative. This principle is another important part of the psychological context for learning and thus something that teachers need to attend to when creating the best possible setting for learning to take place. There's a trap in teaching which is very easy to fall into – that of neglecting to look at the task from the novice learner's point of view so as to make the demands of the task readily comprehensible to the learner. A simple way to avoid the trap is to apply the CWAK test – CWAK stands for Clear When Already Known – in other words what you need to know (and use) is only clear once you know it and not clear whilst you are learning it. Applying the CWAK test to the CWAK trap means looking at the task from the novice learner's point of view as far as we can. This isn't always easy as we often forget the process we went through to learn something once we have mastered it – an example is that you probably don't recall much of the detail of how you learned to read since once you can read you don't need to use the process of learning any further. Applying the CWAK test as a teacher means consciously asking yourself questions like 'What will I be asking children to do in this task, and what must they already be able to do to be successful'.

An amusing example of the importance of using the novice learner's point of view comes from the classroom of a student-teacher in her second substantial teaching practice. The class was Year 5 and the intention was that the children would learn about the water cycle. The student began with a classic CWAK tactic 'Today we are going to learn about the water cycle'. Now, since an introduction is supposed to allow the audience to prepare for what's coming, that statement assumes that children already know what those words mean. The student discovered that at least one child was very confused when after the student's drawing of the water cycle on the board had been quickly described without any explanation of why the concept of *cycle* was important, the student instructed the children to 'Do your own drawing of the water cycle'. Imagine the confusion and dismay on all sides when one boy, not known for rebellion, produced a drawing of a frog (link with water) on a bike (cycle)!

So the moral of the story is avoid the CWAK trap. Make sure that *you* and *your pupils* are clear about what the task involves from the outset. This doesn't mean that every learning opportunity has to be cut and dried. Far from it! There's obvious value in enabling children to find their own way through some tasks, but they need to know that that is the approach they should take. Get used to thinking very carefully about the words you use to tell children what kinds of learning process are involved in the work. Review the range of terms you could/should use when setting children off to work so that you really do say (or write, if it's a workcard or sheet) what you mean. If you mean … Listen, read carefully, memorise, compare, invent, recall, adapt, … all processes of dealing with information/skills, then you must say so, otherwise the pupils will be left victims of the CWAK trap. Now, fortunately most people are quite good at putting up with lack of clarity in their information world and most of us get by most of the time, but there are risks involved. We may get the wrong end of the stick (remember the frog on the bicycle), we may waste time and energy and we may be left feeling rather foolish or cross. You know that classroom learning has to be more secure than that so, to avoid confusions, waste of time and energy and loss of self-composure (on both sides?), take time at the outset to be clear about your intentions and to express them clearly.

Helping children to know what and how they are learning

Don't be afraid to use the appropriate labels for learning processes even with young children. After all we are quite confident in teaching children early on that a three-sided shape is called a 'triangle' so why not talk about 'comparing', 'adapting', 'reviewing' and so on, when these are the processes we want children to develop and use *because* they are important in achieving a successful and satisfying outcome. A good example of how lack of clarity can be unhelpful occurs quite often in some classrooms. A child finishes a fairly complex piece of work, say a story, and brings it to the teacher. The teacher advises the child to go back and 'Read it through' or to 'Check it'. Dutifully, the child does read through their work but if they don't already know that the advice *really* means 'Read it through looking out for spelling mistakes, words missed out, words you might like to change…', then they will not do what the teacher intends and may appear to be less successful than they could be. So, we return to a now familiar theme, work out what it is you intend children to do, plan how you will support them in doing it and give very clear information and support when they are working.

Another example of how teachers can help children to develop good 'learning to learn' skills comes from the sphere of memory. You will know how often we call upon children to use their memory – for facts, for incidents, for reactions – and yet we seem to give relatively little attention to helping them to develop an efficient memory. It is known that the youngest children in school will have only a very hazy idea of what it means to learn in the sense of memorising. However, they will already be very familiar with the idea of remembering. In other words, they are already good at a fairly passive version of memory use, but need to develop the capacity for the conscious act of committing information to memory. Given the instruction 'Don't forget to…' or 'Remember to bring…' children up to Y2 or so will generally be quite confident that they will have no problem with such an instruction *and* that they won't have to *do* anything to comply with it. Actually, of course, their confidence is often ill-founded and they do not remember particularly well if the information is not particularly clear or especially important – numerous sets of PE kit and reading books left at home will testify to this!

As they get older, most children will gradually realise that there are ways that they can work with their memory – psychologists call these 'strategies': ways like writing something down, pairing the point-to-be-remembered with something already very familiar, asking someone else to remind them, writing something on the back of one's hand and so on. The important point in all this for the teacher is that children can be helped to develop good strategies earlier and more effectively if they are demonstrated and explained to them *and* if there are plenty of opportunities to keep practising them. In this sense using memory well, as an example of a 'learning to learn' skill, is like many other skills – it improves with practice.

In the well-ordered classroom – that is one in which every aspect of the context gives the maximum possible support to the children's full development – such clear and consistent reference to effective ways of tackling work will be part of the fabric of the whole enterprise. For example, children will be introduced at the beginning of the year to the way in which the teacher wants them to tackle certain tasks and these ways will be very publicly supported by the teacher until they become familiar to the children. Even after this point the teacher will still take time to remind and reinforce in low-key ways so the children have a good chance of meeting the teacher's expectations and requirements without nagging or trial and error.

There is an approach to helping children to track down correct spellings which fits this model. It is inevitable that children of any age will want to use words in their work which they do not know how to spell, or do not feel confident about, so the wise teacher works out a procedure which the children can use. Via such procedures, for instance, we can avoid finding them trailing around the classroom after any available adult, with pencil and paper or word book which they proceed to put under the adult's nose, saying 'Stegosaurus' or some such thing. A much more effective approach is to work out a series of steps which the child *knows* (because you have taught them) they should go through. For instance, depending on the age of the child, the procedure might include steps like:

1 Say the word over to yourself so that you really listen to the sounds in it.
2 What is the first sound? Think about the letter which matches that sound.
3 Think if you've used the word before – look in your word book.
4 Examine word lists displayed in the room (because the teacher also uses this technique to support the learning of word or sound families and to record the 'specialist' vocabulary encountered in a particular topic).
5 Check in the word book/dictionary which is kept on your table.

6 Ask *one* person sitting at your table.
7 Only if none of these steps produces a result should you ask the teacher or other adult.

This may sound quite off-putting but it need not be if well taught. Most of all, it fulfils a number of important functions which are part of the general ethos of the effective learning environment. It encourages children to try for themselves first, to take an organised approach to solving a problem and to avoid disturbing the work of others until they are entitled to. Notice too, that it is an opportunity to use and exemplify in practice those labels for processes which we were thinking about earlier – 'listen', 'think', 'examine', 'check'. The great thing about introducing children to such processes in such a way is that children quickly discover that they work and so will feel supported in being more effectively involved in their own learning.

Comfort in the psychological context

This idea of the importance of children feeling supported is another aspect of the psychological context to which teachers need to pay attention. In some way or another all new learning involves some level of risk for the learner – quite often the learner will actually recognise that there is a risk and enjoy it, as for instance when people decide to learn some new skill which they know that they will find difficult. Psychologists have studied the ways in which individuals differ in terms of how much risk they can deal with effectively, that is, tolerate, until they reach a satisfying outcome. It turns out that the individual's capacity to deal with risk is a complicated business involving personality characteristics, the person's previous experience, the type of reward which will come with success and the chance which the person believes they have of being successful. Even very cautious people will be prepared to have a go if the situation is somewhat familiar, the reward is a good one and the chance of success is high. Think about your own reactions to such a situation – and to the opposite end of the scale, where you have no relevant experience, the reward is a mystery and you feel very little confidence in your chance of succeeding, maybe because you don't even know what success is! Would you have a go? Sad to say there are times for many children when they are put in this position in terms of school learning. Because of the CWAK trap, it's difficult for them to know what the task is, the reward may not have been clearly signalled or is one they're not sure that they want anyway, and the chance of success is low – in fact they have previous experience of failure and daily see others fail all around them. No wonder that some children don't want to get involved in this process and we see them using all kinds of avoiding behaviours ranging from the time-wasting pencil sharpening to outright refusal to begin or to continue the task. We know that children will differ in terms of how they respond to situations involving risk and so, as teachers, we need to take account of that knowledge in how we organise life in our classrooms. This means doing our best to give clear information about the routines and procedures which surround the actual point of the learning – so that, for instance, the child who is tackling a difficult piece of new learning in maths is not also worrying about how to set out the work. In this circumstance the effective teacher will have addressed the potential problem, perhaps by advising the child on layout in advance or by reassuring the child that layout can be sorted out once they've worked through the new task. The important point is that we want to encourage children to feel 'brave' about new learning so that they will tackle tasks they feel might be difficult. Equally we want them to put their intellectual energies into the real point of the learning and not be distracted or undermined by wondering about less currently important aspects of the task.

A common example of how teachers try to reduce the feeling of difficulty (and thus the sense of risk) is the way in which children writing the first draft of a story will be encouraged to concentrate on their ideas and their expression leaving attention to completely accurate spelling and punctuation to later stages in the drafting process. The point which makes this classroom procedure really effective is that children have to know *how* it works and believe *that* it works; that, for instance, somebody won't criticise their handwriting at an early draft stage. So we are back to the concept of the well-ordered classroom where every aspect of the context gives the maximum support to the children's full development – in this case the procedures will have been identified by the teacher before contact with the class, will have been clearly introduced to the children with ample opportunity to learn the procedure without risk, and will be consistently reinforced through repeated use. After this the children, whatever their individual tendency to accept risk, will be much more likely to have a go and to actually enjoy taking a chance. In such a climate teachers can encourage children to try out new ways of working, to tackle open-ended tasks, to experiment and so on – the technique of group drafting of material which young children so enjoy is a good example of a supportive learning climate. In such a climate children will feel more at ease in taking intellectual chances and in dealing with failure when it occurs. It is crucial to the learning process that children are able to accept the full range of outcomes between total success and a relative shambles because that way they will really learn from their experience. The message has to be that not always succeeding is no great disaster because you can always try again, in the supportive classroom, where trying is the most rewarded behaviour, rewarded by clear signals of approval from adults and other children alike. The effective classroom has a generous feel about it within which children feel psychologically safe and brave. This is not easy to build from scratch but it is within the grasp of every teacher and within the entitlement of every pupil.

To extend your thinking about this idea of risk-taking and its effect on children's learning, wait for the next time you hear a child say 'Do we have to do this?' or 'This is boring'. At that point look for as much information as you can about the contexts for learning. Does the child actually know what to do? What has been their previous experience of such learning situations? Does the child know what a successful outcome actually means and what will follow from it? Might they feel they don't really want the 'reward'? Asking these kinds of questions may enable you to see that the real message which the child is sending is to do with feeling confused and at intellectual and emotional risk – and which one of us is happy to proceed in those circumstances? (Of course there's always the chance that the task really is boring and then it's up to the teacher to find another way to cover the ground!)

Responding to individual differences

At this stage it will be helpful to your understanding of the importance of the psychological context if you bear in mind that the range of individual learner characteristics is considerable – we have looked at learning style, task understanding and tolerance of uncertainty and risk as particular aspects of individual difference. You will also know that there are other differences to do with age and ability – these are not covered here as there are many good textbooks which you can use to augment your knowledge. Section 1 contains some references which you could use.

You should also bear in mind that particular characteristics can influence each other in the individual in particular situations, and so it is probably unrealistic to think that the teacher could expect to form *watertight* predictions about what will happen at any one point in time. The sensible approach for the teacher is to ensure that they know as much as possible about the *likely* range of differences within the particular age group they are teaching, then to take account of information which they have about specific children in the class and then to strive to present material to all the children as clearly as they can, in a variety of ways and speeds, so that every child will have an optimum chance to make progress. This approach to planning and teaching at the whole class level will then allow the teacher to make more finely-tuned decisions in the case of specific children at specific times or with specific types of material.

In a nutshell, there is no substitute for knowing as much as you can about the psychological development of children in general and about the specific intellectual strengths of your pupils in particular. In that way you will be most aware of what you need to do in order to arrange the best psychological context in your classroom.

THE SOCIAL CONTEXT

Whenever you have spent any time in a classroom where the children were present you could not have failed to observe the many and varied social interactions that took place between and amongst the children and the adults in the room. You will also have noticed that these interactions were important to the people concerned because they gave time to them and showed through various aspects of their behaviour, for instance their body language, that they were putting emotional energy into them.

Social interaction is very important to all humans and the skills it involves begin to develop very early in childhood. By the time children come to school they will already have developed friendships and will quite possibly show that they don't get on easily with some people. Within the general framework of the classroom system which we are considering in this chapter, the role of the social context, of which social interactions form a substantial part, is very important because it can be seen to have considerable effects on the quality of learning which takes place in the classroom. The task of the teacher in terms of the social context is to understand how it affects learning and how they can make the most effective use of that knowledge in practical classroom planning and management. Activity 2 in Section 2 (pp. 35–6) sets out some ways in which you can observe and record social interaction.

We have already met some relevant ideas in earlier parts of the chapter, for instance, how the layout of the classroom can signal the types of social exchange which is expected. Another relevant idea which we have already explored is that the place where teachers allow/require certain children to work can send signals about how these children are viewed; this will affect the children's status in other children's eyes and probably also affect the patterns of social interaction in the class. In some cases, teachers will let friends sit together – or not sit together – depending on whether friendly interaction is thought to help or hinder the learning outcomes. Children become aware of what these working positions mean at an early stage in their school career and will sometimes behave in a prejudiced way towards the children who work in them.

We have also seen how learning involves risk and that some children are less ready to take risks than others – although they may be more inclined to 'have a go' in a pair or a group as they gain confidence from 'braver' classmates. Teachers can find this aspect of social support very useful in helping them to decide on groups and activities.

Social interaction is an influential aspect of classroom life which the teacher must be aware of, but they must also see that they have a role in influencing social interaction and the social development of their pupils. After any prolonged contact with children in a classroom we will be able to recall some who are very shy and dislike working intensively with other children, or children who are quite aggressive and have difficulty in getting on with their fellow learners. There will obviously be individual differences in how children handle the social aspects of the classroom but, whilst allowing for such differences, it is important that teachers promote good social development in children. The classroom environment is an excellent setting in which children can acquire and develop the range of social skills which are involved in being able to get on with others and to be more successful as individuals and in groups. This requires good cooperation between all of the people involved in the classroom enterprise – adults and children.

If you spend a few minutes reflecting on what 'cooperation' means in the setting of the classroom you will identify the social skills of sharing and helping, the ability to learn from others without resentment and to accept constructive criticism and the capacity to put up with others because the goal is more important than personal preferences. It also means being able to work without prejudices based on gender or cultural differences or differences in physical and intellectual ability. It is a major part of the teacher's professional responsibility to see that they must plan and organise learning experiences for their pupils so that such cooperation becomes a part of each child's social development. In the section on 'discipline' (pp. 32–3) you will find reference to some current issues in the general management of children's behaviour which impinge upon their social interactions in the classroom and also further reading on the subject in the bibliography. You will also find references to books which will give you further information about the impact of the social context beyond the classroom – the school, the family and the community.

When teachers think about social interaction in the classroom and how they might influence it, they often think of how they can arrange the working groups within the class. In some classes the teacher allows the children to choose who they work with, in other classes the teacher always chooses and in yet other classes a mixture of pupil choice and teacher choice is used. Sometimes the organisation of the groups is virtually unchanging over quite long periods, say a term, sometimes the groups are reorganised very frequently and sometimes a combination exists where, for instance, groups for mathematics change very little whereas groups for drama are different each week. There can be no hard and fast rules which say that any particular kind of organisation is always superior, including whether groups will be more effective than individual working; as we have seen elsewhere in this chapter, what matters is that the teacher has thought through the organisation which is used and can justify it in terms of the support for learning which it will provide. It is also important that the teacher is prepared to share the justifications with the pupils so that, for instance, in a particular session children who usually sit together really know why they have been asked to work in different locations. At the simplest level this open approach will limit the chance of children protesting and diverting attention from the real purpose of the session.

It is important to give careful thought to the size of group which you will organise for various activities so that each child will have the optimum setting within which to meet your learning intentions, and remember that more groups generally means more demands on your attention.

There are many aspects to bear in mind when deciding on the size, composition and 'lifespan' of any particular style of organisation. It is important to be clear about the function within the learning topic which the organisation is intended to fulfil. Whatever organisation you decide upon, you must get to know as much as you can about the social development of children in general, particularly in the age group which you are planning for, you must spend time getting to know your pupils in a variety of settings during the school day and you must build this knowledge into your forward planning, using it as you review the outcomes of the various teaching/learning sessions.

You will find the questions in Activity 3 in Section 2 (pp. 36–8) will help you to use your knowledge of the social context to contribute to a well-ordered classroom.

CONCLUSION

This chapter began with a description of the classroom in use as a highly complex and fascinating system. We have seen that physical, psychological and social aspects of the system have a great influence on learning and that teachers must take account of these aspects in their planning and teaching.

You will also know from experience that classrooms are places where many things go on at the same time and where unpredicted and unexpected things happen – all adding to the complexity of the system – so there is a great deal to think about in attempting to create the well-ordered classroom which has been referred to several times within the chapter.

SECTION 1: BACKGROUND

Some classroom layouts for you to consider

Think about these arrangements of furniture in terms of the elements of the use of space which have been referred to in the chapter.

1. A typical 'social' seating arrangement

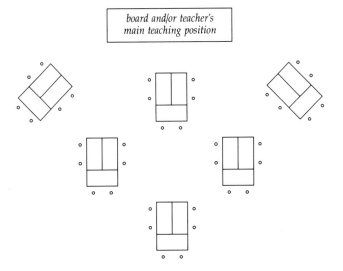

2. A simple variation to facilitate sustained, individual seatwork.

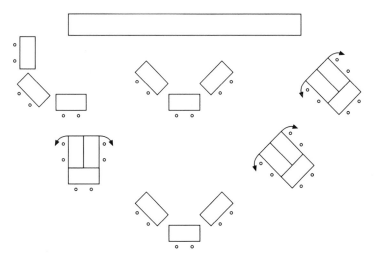

By simply swinging the 'facing' tables outward, the children's main lines of sight are no longer directly on the faces/work of their immediate neighbours.

3. How about this! Several teachers have experimented with this style and have found it to be dramatically successful in focusing children's attention on the particular task in hand, whether that was individual seatwork or shared activities.

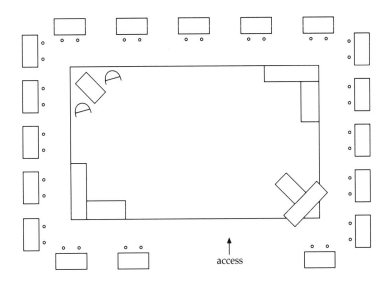

access

Children carry out their sustained, individual seatwork at the tables around the periphery of the layout. Discussion work is done on the carpeted area in the middle which is fringed by low storage facilities and tables for display or work needing particularly spacious flat surfaces.

This layout has a few essential features if it is to work. The classroom area must have clear boundaries against which individual workspaces can be placed. Each pupil's frequently-used equipment must be stored at or alongside their workspace or must be in some very portable container. There must be adequate and appropriate storage facilities which must be low enough to allow the teacher clear sight of children wherever they are and vice versa. The teacher must have thought through this layout and the resulting procedures very carefully in advance and must be prepared to introduce the situation to children with care and understanding as they will be quite surprised and excited at the initial novelty of it.

You can read about how one teacher employed this approach in the paper by Lucas (1990), which is listed in the Bibliography for this chapter. In particular, you could consider the section on pages 91 and 92 of the paper where Lucas sets out the design of the approach.

Discipline in schools

At various points in Chapter 2 we have used the notion of the well-ordered classroom as one in which every aspect of the context gives the maximum possible support to the children's full development. A number of studies of the management of children's behaviour in schools and classrooms have shown that the dimension of 'order' is very important.

For instance, in 1988 the (then) DES set up a Committee of Enquiry into 'Discipline in Schools' to be chaired by Lord Elton. The Committee was given the task of considering 'what action can be taken … to secure the orderly atmosphere necessary in schools for effective teaching and learning to take place' (Committee of Enquiry, 1989: 54). Amongst an extensive list of recommendations made in 'The Elton Report', are a number which are of particular relevance to student-teachers, their tutors and mentors.

As well as reading sections of the Report itself, you will find useful information in a book of papers called *Discipline in Schools* and edited by Wheldall (1992) – full details of the book are given in the Bibliography for this chapter. The first chapter of that book is an introduction to the Report by the Vice-Chair of the Elton Committee and is very helpful in setting the report in context and in outlining some main themes. The second chapter by Merrett and Wheldall will also be of interest to you since it is about 'Teacher training and classroom discipline'. Other chapters in the book will provide you with information and – equally important – will provoke you to think about how *you* can maintain an orderly and supportive classroom ethos when you are in the role of teacher.

Within the context of this book we can pick out some ideas from The Elton Report and subsequent commentaries upon it.

Many studies have noted that inexperienced teachers generally feel ill-prepared to cope with difficult classroom behaviour because they have seen an insufficient focus in their training on the particular skills necessary for effective classroom management. Dealing effectively with challenges in classroom management is not a single competence which suddenly emerges in the teacher. Rather it is a constellation of ideas and responses which builds up as teachers gain in classroom experience and it is the *active* use of such experience which strengthens the development of the repertoire of appropriate teacher action. Making sense of our experiences so that we can learn from them and actively use them, is a major life task for each one of us and the early experiences of difficulties in classroom management can be particularly difficult to make sense of. The inexperienced teacher is often left feeling incompetent and vulnerable by the recollection of unpleasant events. When such difficulties occur, the teacher is often not really sure what actually happened and may feel that they responded before they had time to think or that they didn't respond nearly quickly enough. No type of training can guarantee that such episodes will not occur, so it is important to see how they can be used as learning opportunities for beginning teachers. The conscious step of reflecting on events is the vital starting point in the learning process and the help and support of tutors, mentors and student colleagues to reinforce and extend the recollection of events is crucial. It is also very important to develop the readiness to use the process of self-appraisal as a constructive, professional approach and Chapter 6 will help you to do this.

Most difficult behaviour in schools has highly complex origins. These will include the way in which the child feels willing and able to tackle the challenge of the work presented, the ways in which teachers respond to children's needs for direct support in their work and the ways in which a school as a functional whole views acceptable behaviour and deals with unacceptable behaviour. Dealing with difficult behaviour cannot be laid at the door of any one of these strands alone. The whole package involves good preparation by teachers of learning tasks which are interesting and achievable by each pupil, presented within a supportive and stimulating classroom atmosphere where pupils understand the risks and rewards, all set in a school ethos which values effort and a sense of community from all participants whether they are children or adults. Each of the chapters in this book sets out to support beginning teachers and their advisers as they embark on the development of the professional repertoire of the effective teacher.

As well as general approaches to creating and maintaining the well-ordered classroom, such as stem from the Elton Report, there are several, more specific, approaches which you could consider in the light of your particular teaching experiences and opportunities. One is the 'Positive Teaching' approach which has resulted from a long-running study into effective classroom behaviour management based at the Centre for Child Study at the University of Birmingham. The main researchers, Wheldall and Merrett, have described briefly the approach in a chapter in the book edited by Wheldall (1992), which was referred to earlier. It is well worth reading and discussing with those involved with you in School Experience.

Another thought-provoking approach is advocated by Rogers (1990) who argues that orderliness cannot be achieved in schools by an imposed system of control which ignores the pupils' close involvement in their own decisions about behaviour. You can guess the main theme of Rogers' approach from the title of his book – *You Know The Fair Rule* – and will be able to link it to those aspects of this chapter which have emphasised the need for children to *understand* what is being asked of them, whether this relates to learning or behaviour.

You should also move on to consider a specific aspect of indiscipline which has attracted much public attention and concern – that of bullying. The book by Elliott (1991) in the Bibliography sets out to help all those who are involved with children's welfare to develop ways of dealing with bullying at the individual, group and school level.

SECTION 2: ACTIVITIES

Activity 1

As you start on the following information-gathering exercise begin by thinking about a classroom which you know.

When first encountering the classroom space in which you are to work there are several things you can take note of. While the room is empty of people, look for the 'fixed' points which you will need to take into account and will not be able to modify much, if at all. For example, note the position of the electric sockets, the water supply, the windows, the radiators, the coat pegs, the storage for lunch boxes, the display space and so on.

At this stage make a plan of the classroom, roughly to scale and mark these fixed points on it. (Take a leaf out of the kitchen designer's book and use squared paper.) Make several copies of this plan of the 'empty' room so that you can add further details later.

Next, think about the furniture. Mark the current position of the various items on one copy of your plan, as close to scale as you can. It will be handy to have several copies of this version too.

The next stage involves looking at the classroom in use at various stages of the many activities which will take place in it. Start with the regular routines of children entering and leaving the room *en masse*, look at how they move around the room when they are not specifically guided by the teacher or by task demands, e.g. first thing in the morning, as each child goes to their desk or tray and then to a position in which to wait for the teacher to begin the morning proceedings. At this stage you may be able to see whether the physical type and arrangement of the furniture within the fixed aspects of the classroom have any effect, useful or adverse, on children's behaviour. For instance, you may notice that when most children are on their feet there are real traffic jams in some areas, or that some children cannot really settle in their own place until somebody else has got settled in theirs. We'll come back to the implications of this kind of situation later but, for now, mark these movement patterns and clusters on the plan of the furnished classroom. Don't make this too elaborate at this stage – you might just mark any route or location which you think seems to cause a hitch in the proceedings.

The next version(s) of your plan of the furnished classroom could relate to specific sessions or types of activities. For instance, you could begin by listing some contrasting situations in terms of what the occupants of the classroom are doing and where they are working. You could think about:

- a practical session where children are working individually and mostly each in their own workspace, but there is scope for quite a lot of social interaction, e.g. for an art activity

- a practical session where children are working in small groups and some movement is involved, say, to collect and return equipment

- a lesson where each child is closely involved in an extended task sitting in their own workspace, e.g. silent reading

- a lesson where the proceedings and the pace are being led by the teacher and children are expected to pay close attention to what is being said or shown, e.g. a story session

Your particular list will depend greatly on the age of the children in the class you are thinking about and on the kinds of preferences the school has for specific classroom arrangements. We would not expect very young pupils to spend long periods sitting and working alone, so that example may not fit your particular classroom 'test-pad'. Equally, it may be that the classroom you are thinking about is laid out in topic/subject areas and it is very rare for the whole class to gather around the teacher for any length of time. The point of the exercise here is for you to bring to mind some fairly familiar situations which you can then analyse in terms of the way in which facilities, including use of space, have a bearing on the learning outcomes.

Having compiled a brief list, take each example and think about where each of the participants needs to be in order to work effectively, how they get there, how they move around within the space while they are working and how they move away at the end of the session. It may help you to look at one of your copies of the plan of the furnished classroom so that you have a 'bird's eye view' of the movement patterns. As has already been suggested, you could mark the main movement patterns and clusters for each of the different kinds of situations which you have decided to include in your list.

The final step in this information-gathering exercise is to think about the type of session where several kinds of activity are going on simultaneously; for example, some children are sitting at individual and silent work, others are working quietly in groups, others are working individually but moving around and making considerable noise (e.g. hammering nails in a Technology project), and others are involved with the adult(s) in the room on work requiring interaction and concentration. You may not have seen such a session in your 'test-pad' classroom but it should not be difficult to imagine this by looking at your plan of the furnished room and adding on your visualisation of these various activities.

Activity 2

The following material provides some ideas for ways of observing and recording social interaction in the classroom.

The simplest way of recording a child's behaviour is to observe the child closely over a period of time and to note down everything that the child does during that period. When this observation and recording stage is complete you can then go over the entries and sort them into various categories – for example, playing alone, playing with other children, watching other children, talking to an adult, and so on.

This simple record will tell you what a child has been doing but not how much time they have spent doing it. That kind of record requires a slightly more complex form of recording. For example, you can start out with an A4 sheet on which you have already listed thirty-second intervals and then you note down at each interval exactly what your 'target' child is doing: 00.00 Nareema begins puzzle; 00.30 Asks Penny for help; 1.00 Still watching Penny; 1.30 Talking to Anjali while building the puzzle, and so on. When your observation period is complete you can calculate how much time a child has spent working alone or cooperating with another child or disputing over equipment, etc. Incidentally, this type of recording technique can be very useful in showing how much time a child spends on and off task and also what triggers the change from on-task to off-task behaviour. This information could help you to devise more supportive working conditions for a particular child.

To return to the recording of social interaction. You could decide that you want to record the interaction in a group and then you would have to use the continuous recording technique suggested above – but you might make the task more manageable by having a prepared matrix which shows the children's names along rows and types of interaction as column headings. Then, each time a particular child demonstrates a particular kind of behaviour, you would put a mark in 'their' box. By this means you would be able to see, for example, that particular children more frequently initiate a particular type of play or intervene and disrupt the play of others.

If the behaviour in which you are interested has strong verbal components, then you could use a tape recorder as a second source of information. Two pieces of advice, though: classrooms are quite noisy places and tape recorders register all the sounds whatever their significance, so you can end up with quite a cacophony. Try putting the recording machine on a soft surface, maybe a small stack of books, to limit the amount of vibration it picks up. Second, if you are recording a group, you still need to take contemporaneous notes so that, later, you will know who said what!

There are many ways of recording social interaction and you will find some suit you more than others. You will get more accurate with practice, in the sense that your entries will be more focused or more complete, and your records will become more useful as you become more clear about what you are looking for. Becoming a good observer is a useful skill for teachers – and that includes being an unobtrusive observer, so get to it and practise!

Activity 3

The following questions will enable you to review a range of contextual factors based on the material in the chapter. Use the questions as you plan, for instance at the early stage of collecting your ideas together and again at the stage when you have your plan of action worked out in detail.

Physical context

1 Does the planned layout of the working space match my intentions for teaching/ learning approaches?
   THINK ABOUT: separating clean and messy areas; quiet and noisy activities; good lines of sight for the children and for you; easy routes for movement as necessary for the children and for you.

2 Will the arrangement of working space send appropriate signals to children about the kinds of learning which have been planned for?
   THINK ABOUT: the need to avoid conflict between seating patterns and working methods.

3 Will each child and adult have easy access to resources and sufficient space to work effectively?
   THINK ABOUT: the location of equipment which will be needed; specific facilities for children with special needs; individual/shared working space; suitably sized furniture.

The psychological context

1 Will individual children's learning styles mesh with the teaching approach I plan to use?
   THINK ABOUT: appropriate working pace/tempo; varied presentation of the route to the goal (steps and overall picture).

2 Will children be able to identify what their tasks are and will they be able to recognise when they are succeeding?
   THINK ABOUT: clear setting out of tasks including reference to strategies for success; giving pointers to success from the outset.

3 Will children know how they can work most effectively in this session?
   THINK ABOUT: signals you send about pace and useful strategies; supporting during the session without nagging; ensuring that the teaching approach is consistent with the teaching/learning intentions.

4 Am I asking all or some children to take risks which they might feel uncomfortable with – how and when will I support them?
   THINK ABOUT: individual children's levels of competence; individual children's tolerance of novelty and uncertainty; the need to give clearly available rewards for quality effort – rewards which children value.

The social context

1 Have I planned the organisation of individual or group work to take account of children's social needs?

THINK ABOUT: your aim to help individual children to develop their interpersonal skills in particular ways, e.g. to cooperate.

2 Have I given thought in my planning of time to my social interactions with children?

THINK ABOUT: your role as active facilitator of learning; your role in helping children to be confident in interacting with adults.

3 Will children know what I am expecting in terms of routines and procedures for working as individuals or groups, or will I have to plan time for explaining these and for supporting children as they use them?

THINK ABOUT: giving reasons for the organisation which you have planned; respecting children's preferences for particular organisations as far as possible in your decisions.

BIBLIOGRAPHY

Committee of Enquiry into Discipline in Schools (1989) *Discipline in Schools. Report of the Committee of Enquiry chaired by Lord Elton*, DES.

Dunne, E. and Bennett, N. (1990) *Talking and Learning in Groups*, Routledge.

Elliott, M. (1991) *Bullying: A Practical Guide to Coping for Schools*, Longman.

Fontana, D. (1987) *Psychology for Teachers*, BPS/Macmillan (particularly pp. 241–6).

Gulliford, R. and Upton, G. (eds) (1992) *Special Educational Needs*, Routledge.

Lucas, D. (1990) 'Systems at work in the primary classroom – a retrospective study of classroom layout', in Frederickson, N. *Soft Systems Methodology: Practical Applications in Work with Schools*, University College London.

Meadows, S. (1986) *Understanding Child Development*, Hutchinson.

Nisbet, J. and Shuksmith, J. (1986) *Learning Strategies*, Routledge.

OFSTED (1993) *Well Managed Classes in Primary Schools: Case Studies of Six Teachers*, DFE.

Rogers, B. (1990) *You Know the Fair Rule: Strategies for Making the Hard Job of Discipline in Schools Easier*, Longman.

Tizard, B. (1988) *Young Children at School in the Inner City*, Open Books.

Wheldall, K. (ed.) (1992) *Discipline in Schools: Psychological Perspectives on the Elton Report*, Routledge.

Wragg, E.C. (1993) *Class Management*, Routledge.

3 PLANNING FOR LEARNING

In this chapter you will:

- identify intentions for children's learning

- understand the important aspects of planning a teaching session

- recognise the importance of integrating assessment procedures into the planning process

- consider the debate which exists about the topic versus subject approach to planning in primary schools

- differentiate between short-, medium- and long-term planning

- be introduced to a model for medium-term planning

DEVELOPING INTENTIONS FOR CHILDREN'S LEARNING

No planning can take place without a clear idea, on the part of the teacher, of what the children in the class are going to learn. The National Curriculum lays the parameters for you here but it will always be your responsibility to be sure about your intentions for learning within those broad parameters. Imagine for the moment that within your class you will be using the topic of 'mini beasts' as a vehicle to develop work in the areas of Science, English and Geography. The decision has been taken by the school because of the easy access to first-hand experience (a nature area which has been developed in the school grounds) for the children and because of the potential of that topic for delivery of particular identified aspects of the National Curriculum. Consider what you may want the children to know about mini beasts, for example, What do particular creatures look like? Where do they live? or, how may the topic be used as a vehicle for children's learning, for example, What are the elements of a useful description? How may you show the differences between different sorts of beasts? How do these questions match with the curriculum areas which have been identified for this class at this stage? You will want to look carefully at the National Curriculum expectations which have been allocated for consideration with this class. These will offer generalised statements to guide your planning, but you will need much more detail in order to identify intentions for learning in a single teaching session. The associated content requirements will give some help here.

Assume that Geography has been identified as a focus at this time with the emphasis on:

- Observing and talking about a familiar place
- Naming familiar features of the local area

At Key Stage 1 children may be expected to:

- identify and name familiar features
- discuss and explain their likes and dislikes about features

To do this they will need to:

- observe
- measure
- sketch

It is with this information and a knowledge of the school environment, especially the nature area which has been built, that you will be able to identify specific learning intentions for a series of teaching sessions. The intentions for a single session will not be a restatement of the general aims, they will instead identify one step towards its achievement as well as other things which you and the children will want to learn. The same procedures will apply to the work in Science and English, and the relationships between these curriculum areas may be explored.

PLANNING TEACHING SESSIONS

What does a lesson plan need to do? It will identify:

- objectives for the session
- learning experiences and activities, including their sequence
- the teachers's role in the learning
- resources for learning
- assessment indicators

Objectives: Set out the learning intentions for the children, i.e. *what* the children will learn.

Learning experiences/activities: Show how the learning will be achieved, i.e. *what* activities you will provide for the children. Show a detailed pathway through the lesson, including the management of time available, i.e. *how* you provide a structure for the learning experiences.

Teacher's role: Show the actions which will be taken by the teacher to ensure that learning takes place, i.e. *what* you will do.

Resources: Indicate the materials and equipment which will be needed for the whole session, i.e. *what* you will need for yourself and for the children.

Assessment indicators: Show at what point in the session particular learning objectives are being explored, i.e. *when* the children will be doing the learning. Show what evidence you will be looking for from the children and how you will gather that evidence, i.e. *how* you will know that learning has occurred.

An example of a lesson plan format which covers all these aspects is outlined in Figure 3.1.

Example of planning a teaching session

Now imagine that the classteacher has asked you to carry out a teaching session with soil. This is part of a topic on the local environment and the teacher wants the children to collect soil, compare and contrast different sorts of soil and begin to think about what

TEACHING/LEARNING SESSION			DATE . . . .
Objectives These will indicate the content of learning, *what* you intend the children to learn in terms of: • knowledge and understanding • skills • attitudes			**Identified NC Attainment**
Learning experience/activities	**Teacher's role**	**Resources**	**Assessment indicators**
How the learning will be achieved in the classroom: the nature and organisation of the learning experience and *what* the children will do Indicate sequence: steps and stages of the session	Anticipated teacher action	Resources for *teacher* Resources for *children* Space needed Time needed	Evidence that the learning has been achieved: how the indicators are to be identified by the teacher. Methods of assessment: observation listening questioning examining/analysing – written outcomes – drawings – models – taped discussion, etc.

Figure 3.1 Example of a lesson plan format

grows in different sorts of soil. This would be work for the children for a series of sessions. Let us consider the first of such a series using the format outlined in Figure 3.1, but with the details filled in (see Plan 3.1).

The objectives are:

1 On the basis of observation and previous experience classify soils according to different criteria.
2 Use previous knowledge to make hypotheses.

The intentions for the children's learning are identified briefly under objectives and the pathway through the session is outlined in the first column of Plan 3.1. The outline

Learning experiences	Teacher's role	Resources	Assessment indicators
Observe some examples of soil and share these observations as a class. Classify soils on the basis of the observations and own experience. Recognise significant characteristics of soil. Look, listen, answer questions, volunteer information.	Ask questions. Encourage comment. Help all to share in discussion. Point to the relevant characteristics. Maintain orderly atmosphere.	4 jars of soil. Blackboard. 18 containers, 3 for each group. Spoons. Polythene bags. Fill-in activity in case of rain.	Volunteering information. Changing responses after listening to someone's contribution. Using observation as a basis for comment.
Children go outside in groups to collect soil from different parts of the grounds. Use materials carefully. Take turns. Follow instructions.	Give careful precise instructions. Reinforce appropriate behaviour. Care for safety. Organise groups. Provide equipment. Encourage close observation by asking questions.	Paper to cover tables. Soil in containers. Magnifiers – at least 1 per group – more better. Paper for drawing.	Following instruction. Bringing back right things. Participating. Explaining what they have done.
Children return to the classroom. Get into groups of 4. Use the magnifiers to examine the soil. Make comparisons. Jot down observations in note form.	Make sure everybody knows what to do. Ensure calm atmosphere. Appropriate instructions	Blackboard or white paper.	Correct use of magnifiers. Commenting on the soil. Picking out relevant characteristics. Taking short precise notes. Sharing tasks. Accurate drawing, care, concentration.
Observational drawings. Tidy up.	Give instructions. Record outcomes. Encourage participation.		Showing a sense of responsibility.
Give children time to share drawings within groups. Ask members of each group to offer their classification, comment on qualities of soil: why it is like that, what life it will sustain, match drawings and samples.			Identifying appropriate characteristics. Sharing ideas. Recognising qualities of good recording.

Plan 3.1 Example of a teaching session on 'soil'

includes the activities which have been planned for the children, e.g. looking at the teacher's samples of soil, using magnifiers to examine their own samples. However, to help the teacher focus on the significance of the activities for the children's learning, points for assessment are incorporated into Plan 3.1 in the fourth column. The pinpointing of the teacher's role and the need for certain equipment at a particular stage of the session, enables the teacher to decide in advance where s/he and the equipment should be. You will, already, have considered these important aspects of classroom management in Chapter 2.

The value of this form of planning is that it sets out the different elements of the teaching/learning process and places them alongside one another to show the relationship between them. For example, the role of the teacher will change as the nature of the teaching session changes. The assessment of the children's learning runs alongside the teaching and is not confined to the end of the lesson. Look out for a detailed discussion of assessment in Chapter 5.

DETAILED PLANNING FOR STRUCTURE IN A LEARNING SESSION

At times an even more detailed planning format may be helpful. For example, when you are planning a session for the first time or planning for an activity which is new in your teaching repertoire, the type of planning described above may not have enough detail either to help you work through all the aspects of the teaching in advance or, to offer enough reminders about what should come next during the teaching session itself.

First, it is helpful to think about a teaching session having different stages each with an appropriate teacher role.

Introduction: beginning the activity

This section of your planning should indicate how you intend to deal with the following aspects:

- Getting the children's attention: e.g. by making use of teachers signals like 'Are you all ready?', 'I hope you are listening carefully' or starting the activity yourself and making it look extremely interesting. The approach adopted will depend upon the situation and the age of the children.
- Checking that the children are ready: e.g. properly protected (aprons, etc.); nothing in hands as they listen to you; equipment ready to hand.
- Enthusing the children: e.g. reminding them of the interesting aspects or pleasures of the activity; reminding them of some connected activity; telling them about the outcomes of the activity.
- Explaining/introducing the task: e.g. asking questions about an object, artefact or resources; explaining what the activity involves.

Development: keeping the activity going

At this stage you need to consider strategies to keep the children's attention and to anticipate problems:

- ask questions to promote interest and assess understanding
- ensure extra equipment is to hand and positioned to best advantage
- encourage cooperation in the activity and discussion
- consider how individual children may be helped to participate and the less-dominant members encouraged
- offer feedback (encouragement, praise)
- recognise completion of a stage of the session and help to move to the next stage
- encourage friendly social relationships amongst the children

Conclusion: finishing off

At this stage there are two main procedures to plan for:

- Tidying up: knowing where everything has to go; knowing what are the responsibilities of individuals; being able to maintain overall control of all that is going on
- Consolidating and summarising the teaching: establishing opportunities for general

Time	Introduction	Points to remember
e.g. 9.00–9.20	Stimulus? Teaching approach, teaching style? Where will the children be? What is to be their task?	questions to ask, location, use of space.
	Development	
e.g. 9.20–10.15	Class, group, individual working?	How will this be organised?
	What will you be doing to ensure the learning objectives are being addressed?	explanations?
	How will you build on these as necessary to extend learning?	instructions? questions?
	Conclusion	
e.g. 10.15–10.30	This is how you and the children will reflect together on what the children will have learned.	collecting children together, discussing outcomes, has work been collected in?, etc.

Figure 3.2 Detailed lesson plan

discussion of outcomes; knowing what main points should be coming from the teaching; offering feedback to the children

The new format is illustrated in Figure 3.2. If the teaching session on soil were to be re-written in this format, the first stages may look like Plan 3.2. The plan would continue with the detail of tidying up and some of the questions and issues which would need to be considered in the concluding part.

DETAILED PLAN	POINTS TO REMEMBER
Introduction: Beginning the activity	
9.00	
Have the 5 jars on the table at the front but covered up. I have 5 jars here, I wonder if you can guess what is inside them. What do you think? you? you? you?	Remember to ask them to put hands up. Use their names.
Try to describe what this would look like if you were close to it. Now ask someone to come out to the front to check the descriptions.	
Which one is most like the soil in your garden? Can you tell us all anything about the soil? Do you add anything to it? What grows in it?	Check who has a garden. Perhaps talk about the park. Planting bulbs?
Have you noticed soil in different places? On holiday? What was it like?	The red soil in Devon, etc.
This discussion will lead on to classification. Record on blackboard.	Draw some lines beforehand, Colour, texture, content.
Development: Keeping the activity going	
9.30	
Get ready to go out. All the children must know who they are with. Keep in your own group with your own teacher. Tell them which place each will go to. Remind them to watch for instructions from their teacher, because nobody will want to shout.	NB Careful instructions. REPEAT. They will need coats. Send them out a few at a time to get coats. Put them on in the classroom.
Think about others who are working in school as we go out. Walk out altogether, split up only when we get outside. Collect soil. Agree signal for time to come back and where we shall gather to come back in.	Instructions about use of spoons and bags for group and for group leaders.
9.50	
Return quietly. All into classroom, put things down and then, in groups, take coats back. Sitting quietly. Give out equipment and give instructions about covering the tables. Put the soil on to the dishes. Look at it very carefully using the magnifiers. Talk to each other about what you see and then jot down notes. Take it in turn to record what you see.	Instructions about where to put everything. Remind them not to mix up the samples of soil.
Move round the room, talking to groups and individuals, check that they are sketching and remembering to jot down notes.	Check that Ben and Dawn have understood what they have to do. Spend time with Jamie's group until they get started.

Plan 3.2 Example of a more detailed planning format

The value of this format is the space which it offers for you to think through the detailed planning for the session. In the early stages of teaching, the questions which you may *think* will come easily to mind as you work with the children do not always do so. Clearly you will want to be responsive to the children's own contributions but still your pathway through the session needs to be well thought out in advance. Often there are points about which you need to remind yourself. These may be obvious to you as you think in advance, but are easily forgotten in the activity of the session. The second column of Plan 3.2 is a reminder column. It may also be the place where you can pinpoint for yourself some of the assessment activities or the special provision being made for individual children.

PLANNING FOR ORGANISATION OF PARALLEL ACTIVITIES

In the teaching session outlined above the children were all involved in a similar activity. Individuals would learn different things in the course of the session. In the concluding part of the lesson the teacher would reinforce for the children those aspects which s/he intended them to learn, as well as helping them to share individual ideas with each other.

However, in some teaching sessions it would not be appropriate for children to be involved in the same activities. Some of the reasons for this are outlined below:

- that not all the children have the prerequisite knowledge for new activity
- that the teacher wishes to use her time differentially with different groups of children, so that some activities in the classroom must require a minimum of teacher input
- that the needs of the children in terms of ability, aptitude, concentration span make the delivery of a single activity unhelpful
- that expensive equipment is in short supply so that only a small group of children may use it at any one time

An important concept here is differentiation. Children do not learn at the same rate or in the same way. They need different sorts of instruction, different access to the subject matter, varying amounts of practice and reinforcement. Sometimes this may be provided within whole class teaching but at other times it can only be provided by differentiating the learning situation in a more radical way.

The other factors identified above also need to be considered. If an activity requires a substantial teacher input or if the use of certain equipment needs careful supervision or is in short supply, the teacher must manage her/his own time and the children's activities to respond to those needs.

Two illustrations are offered below to show how this might work in practice.

Suppose a teacher is trying to help the children to develop research skills. In presenting this programme of work s/he may have the general aims of:

- helping children to pursue a topic of interest and find the necessary information from reference books and other media
- helping children to be able to analyse the information they find and organise it into a form which makes sense
- showing children how to set out the information they have found in as meaningful and attractive a way as possible

Even a superficial look at those aims shows some of the complexity of the tasks which face children. In using books appropriately children will need to be able to:

- identify which book is relevant
- use the contents page
- use the index
- use pictures for reference
- skim and scan the contents of the pages and paragraphs
- notice similarities and differences

In analysing the material which they have read, children may move from filling in blanks in sentences using appropriate words, through answering questions requiring literal facts and showing relationships between facts to going beyond the information given to formulate hypotheses.

In a primary classroom, children will be at quite different stages in this process of learning, and to give all the same task would leave some seriously floundering and others very bored. There will also be a difference in the amount of teacher attention which children will require in order to be successful. A group of children with learning difficulties are likely to have some problems with reading, with identifying relevant features of text as well as having a need for very frequent teacher feedback as the task progresses in order to maintain motivation. They are likely to start the task with fewer of the prerequisite skills already established. Another group of children, on the other hand, may have many of the skills already within their repertoire and be highly motivated by their interest in the subject matter. Within this context the teacher will need to differentiate in her/his provision in order to ensure progression in the children's learning. The plan for teaching may appear as set out in the following section and Plan 3.3.

Objectives

For group A

1 Pick from a set of books one which will provide information about an identified area.
2 Be able to use the index and contents page to find the appropriate section of the book.
3 Using the identified text, pick out one sentence which answers given questions.

For group B

1 Using two specific texts, find those parts of the texts which relate to the given topic.
2 Summarise the text which has been identified in a way which may be understood by another person.
3 Compare and contrast the information which is given in each text.

For group C

1 Be able to summarise the information which is available in two given texts.
2 Identify information which is necessary to complete task but which is not available in the given texts.
3 Use the evidence from the given texts to hypothesise about the information which is needed.

For all groups

1 Cooperation in completing the task.

The details of this are shown in Plan 3.3.

Plan 3.3 represents an attempt to be responsive to the needs of three different groups of children. The research process is progressive and this progression is shown in the different expectations for the three groups. Group A are working at the basic task of using indexes as well as supplementing rather poor reading skills by using cues. Group B are practising skills already acquired and are concentrating on comparing different accounts of a similar area of study. Group C are expected to be able to go beyond the text as it is written and begin to hypothesise from the evidence available. Their next step will be to decide how they may locate that evidence.

In planning group activities you will need to be well aware of the demands on your own time. In this case the teacher has made a decision to spend most time with the group of children with learning difficulties. The first task for the other two groups needs a common input so children are not required to listen to several sets of instructions. Having spent time with group A the teacher can then be available for the next stage of work for groups B and C. Here, s/he makes use of workcards, since the children are practising skills which they have begun, already, to acquire. In planning for a progressive programme of work you will prepare materials for one group which, eventually, may be used by other groups.

The second illustration in the following section shows group work with much younger children (R/Y1). The group activities extend over the whole day rather than over a teaching session.

Learning experiences	Teacher's role	Resources	Assessment indicators
Remind the class about the topic on Egyptians and the new box of books which has arrived	Motivate the children. Make sure all are involved by asking many to contribute	The new library loan	Notice willingness to join in
Explain that we shall work on a number of activities	Make sure all the children are keen		
Organise the class into the new groups and locate them	Make sure that the children realise this is just for today	List of the groups and where they will sit	Is class still keen?
Ask groups B and C to make up pairs. Ask them to read the workcards. Remind them about how to find the texts and write a summary. Ask them to start work quietly	Make sure they understand the task. Ask for no interruptions while I am with group A	Two texts for each pair	Evidence will show in the written work. Main points raised
Working with A. Using the simpler texts, ask children to make choice of books and explain why. By questioning clarify correct procedures. Review	Give them time to choose and explain choice. Sound out the words	A supply of contrasting books	Active in looking. Using all information and look for cues
Look at the index. If a word is not there think of an alternative which may be used	Keep interest and attention of all		Take part in the task Find other words Show interest
Now move to call together group C, check summary and give out cards with next task related to objectives 2 and 3	Make sure all understand task	Paper Workcards	Identify missing elements correctly Hypothesise and justify hypotheses from the evidence
Call together group B, check summary and explain task related to objectives using a structured sheet which will guide summary	Check summary and deal with difficulties. Make sure they understand	Structured sheet	Correct use of sheet to set out similarities and differences
Return to group A. Review the work and help the group to understand the task and complete successfully	Praise success		Correct identification of sentence Willingness to try and cooperate

Plan 3.3 Example of detailed plan of work for three groups

Objectives

1 To sort various household items according to selected criteria (Mathematics).
2 To build a house from Lego (Technology).
3 To match place mats in structured play area (Mathematics).
4 To write directions from home to school (Geography, English).

For a more detailed scheme, see Plan 3.4.

Plan 3.4 represents a series of activities which children will have to complete during the course of a day. There are a number of activities all of which at some point in time will need teacher input, but some of which are designed for more child independent learning than others. Activities 2 and 3 are specifically designed to be completed with the minimum of teacher input other than appropriate questioning and

Learning experiences	Teacher's role	Resources	Assessment Indicators
Children gathered on carpet to listen to tasks for the day. Establish joint criteria for sorting activity	Explanation of tasks for the day Questioning	Checklists for each activity for children to sign	
Activity 1 Children will sort household items into chosen criteria. Place them in circles drawn on large pieces of paper. If able to, record names under items	Ask questions as to reasons for classification	Large pieces of paper; felt-tip pens	Response to questions How does a response change after listening
Activity 2 Children to build own design of house from Lego bricks	Ask questions about finished outcome. In discussion point to relevant features needed in house structure and need or overlapping joints for stability	Lego bricks – different sizes	Outcome: recognise good and less-good features
Activity 3 Children to play in house corner and set table to match place settings	Questions about place settings	Home corner Place mats marked with knives, forks and spoons	Correct place setting
Activity 4 Children to discuss route to school	Questions Teacher to record key words on flip chart. Model drawing a 'map'	Flip chart Felt-tip	
Children to write out route to school and draw map of route		Paper, pens, crayons	Written outcomes

Plan 3.4 Example of group activities planned over a whole day

observation. Activity 1 demands more teacher input, but this can be done 'on the carpet' with the whole class together and then periodically during the session. Activity 4 is very teacher dependent at the start of the activity and is the focused teaching activity of the session.

The plan shows further relevant features. First, it is clear that some items of equipment (e.g. home area) may be used by limited numbers of children at a time. Second, the structure provides great flexibility to adapt the teaching at any one time or with a particular group to the needs of the children. Third, the longer time-scale is responsive to the needs of young children for time to understand what is expected of them and to explore their own capabilities. In order to build up the concentration span of these young children the teacher will want to build, very much, on their current interests and absorption in an activity. The plan provides enough flexibility for her/him to be able to do that.

THREE LEVELS OF CURRICULUM PLANNING

Up until now we have been concerned with the teacher's daily planning. However, this detailed specific planning is set in the overall planning of the school. The National Curriculum Council (1993) identifies three levels of planning.

Long-term planning is the responsibility of the headteacher and all the staff and is concerned with the whole Key Stage (i.e. 1 or 2). Its purpose is to ensure:

- coverage of the nine subject Orders and Religious Education
- appropriate allocations of time
- coherence, balance and continuity within the whole package
- continuity between Key Stages

Medium-term planning is the responsibility of class teachers supported by subject co-ordinators. Its purpose is to develop detailed plans from the Key Stage plan. These will:

- contain subject-specific units of work
- contain linked units of work
- show sequence in which the units will be delivered
- relate to specific school terms

Short-term planning is the responsibility of class teachers. Its purpose is to ensure that, during each day or week the class will receive:

- a balance of activities based on the medium-term planning
- work differentiated to meet their needs
- a pace of delivery which is appropriate for their needs and as far as possible matches the medium-term plans
- constructive feedback

At the same time the plans will allow for:

- time for teacher assessment
- monitoring and evaluation procedures

SIGNIFICANT FACTORS WHICH UNDERPIN CURRICULUM PLANNING

In the early part of this chapter, a lot of attention has been given to the detail of short-term planning in order to give you the means to work with your class. However, such planning is directed by the long- and medium-term planning of the school. Again it is not possible or useful to cover all aspects at the same time, so in the next sections attention will be focused on medium-term planning with only occasional reference to the long-term level. Before proceeding, it is important to understand some aspects identified by the NCC, listed below, which influence all curriculum planning (NCC 1993).

Allocation of time refers to the process of analysing how time is spent during the school week, term and year and how much of that time will be committed to teaching the National Curriculum subjects.

Continuity refers to the links which will need to be made between subjects and stages in order to achieve coherence across the curriculum for the children.

A continuing unit of work is a 'planned sequence of lessons or activities which relates to an aspect of a single subject' (NCC 1993: 20). In explaining this notion the NCC suggest aspects of mathematics and reading as illustrative examples, where the emphasis is on regular and frequent teaching. In the case of reading, the emphasis is on the development of skills which 'are taught and learned in a progressive and cumulative fashion' (NCC 1993: 20).

A blocked unit of work is a 'distinct and cohesive unit of carefully organised subject content'. Blocked units:

- have a limited, specific time allocation so that they may be fitted into one term
- tend to focus on knowledge and understanding rather than development of basic skills
- focus on a limited range of levels.

Some examples cited by NCC are:

- Science – the structure and function of living things
- Geography – the local area
- English – work based on a particular text

Because of its separate cohesive nature it is possible to locate a blocked unit more flexibly in the termly timetable.

Progression is achieved when subject content is carefully organised into a manageable number of distinct and cohesive units which are sequenced in a meaningful and valid way for the children.

Subject input refers to the need, often reinforced in NCC documents, that the identity and particular character of a subject should be preserved.

MEDIUM-TERM PLANNING

Preparation for medium-term planning

At this stage we are ready to consider the practicalities of medium-term planning for units of work. The latter may spread over a whole term or be completed in half a term – in either case the principles will be the same. Certain assumptions will be made about what has already been decided. That is:

- which subjects will be covered during that term
- the time allocation for the chosen subjects
- whether blocked or continuous units are planned
- some specific content and the potential links which will be allowed between different curriculum areas

For example, a Key Stage 2 class may be studying 'The school in the environment' with related blocked units in History (a local study unit), Geography (especially geographical skills and human geography in a local context) and Technology (especially 'generating a design' and 'planning and making'. At the same time plans may be made for a continuing unit in Maths which is to cover aspects of 'Knowledge and use of numbers, estimation and approximation and the application of number skills in solving problems'. These may be supplemented by blocked and continuing units of work in English, Physical Education, Art and Religious Education.

A model for medium-term planning

Medium-term planning involves two main processes which may themselves be divided up into smaller sections. These processes are described below but are also summarised in diagrammatic form in Figure 3.3.

Stage 1: Identifying and researching a topic/theme

The terms 'topic' and 'theme' are used widely and often their meaning is unclear. In the example in the previous section, the word may refer to a topic around which work is to be organised (in this case 'The school in its environment') or to the theme which is to be addressed within a subject (in this case 'Application of number skills in solving problems'). To avoid confusion the terms will be used in this sense throughout the section. The NCC make quite clear their intention that subject identity should not be lost when work is planned within a topic.

STAGE 1: at stage 1 you need to:

Select ⟶ Inform ⟶ Organise ⟶ Sequence
the topic as a whole

1(i) Identify theme/topic	You will fit into school/class overall NC plan but bring your own ideas to this. Consider relevance in terms of the children's interests, previous experiences, capacity and capacity of theme/topic to offer concrete, first-hand learning from real things.
1(ii) Brainstorm, read around, inform, investigate	Become thoroughly familiar with content subject knowledge. Read around, delve for information at all levels; jot down ideas for activities; play around with draft charts and possible overall sequence.
1(iii) Flow chart showing curriculum areas, outline NC requirements, activities	Organise your ideas into a flow chart showing: • curriculum areas • NC ATs • cross-curricular skills, themes and dimensions + *activities*
1(iv) Identify sequence across topic	Cluster your activities, i.e.: • identify starting point • broad areas to be covered over sets of lessons – possibly weekly or bi-weekly

STAGE 2: at stage 2 you need to:

Work upon each of the curriculum areas as follows:

2(i) Content: relate to NC requirements	What are the key concepts? Establish one/two broad aims. Decide what information, knowledge, understandings you want the children to acquire. You need a fair degree of detail, so that you have the subject matter at your finger-tips. These will become lesson objectives later.
2(ii) Skills and processes of learning	Now look beneath the surface 'content' to determine the learning processes the children will be engaged in. Will they be observing, hypothesising, testing evaluating, reflecting, decision-making, communicating?
2(iii) Sequence/continuity and progression	The sequence of the learning experiences should link and show progression in terms of, for instance: • logical order, e.g. chronology • skill development • increasingly complex tasks/situations • transfer of skills/knowledge
2(iv) Differentiation	Consider which aspects are best suited to certain individuals or groups, which can be tackled by all or most of the children. What do your tasks demand? How can you best prepare and present to match different abilities and needs, including children's special educational needs?

| 2(v) Teaching/learning approaches | Decide the appropriate teaching style for your activities: overall, you should have a balance of class, groups and individual work. List *all* resources needed for scheme. Show those still to be made/obtained! |
| 2(vi) Opportunities for and methods of assessment | State clearly how you intend to
• assess learning
• evaluate your provision
not as a bolt-on, but to clarify assessment techniques in relation to 2(i)–2(v) above. |

Figure 3.3 Model for medium-term planning presented in diagrammatic form
Source: adapted from Morrison, K. and Ridley, K., 1988, p. 140

As we have seen, decisions about the topic/themes may, already, have been made within the school curriculum plan. Alternatively, some flexibility may be possible. Flexibility allows teachers to make use of opportunities which may be available at a particular time of the year, perhaps an exhibition in the town or an interesting feature of the local environment which is of special interest to the class. It also allows more consideration to be given to the needs of the particular class of children. However, too much flexibility will jeopardise the continuity and progression which the whole school plan is intended to ensure.

Having identified the topics/themes, there are the two related processes of exploring the topics/themes and setting out your ideas for activities. All of this will require, first, careful research to make sure that you yourself are as well informed as possible and, second, imagination to think up ideas for activities which will enthuse the children as well as providing a vehicle for ensuring the children's access to the prescribed curriculum areas. At this stage you will be considering the general aims identified for that class in the long-term planning. Your task eventually will be to formulate specific intentions for children's learning related to the relevant NC requirements and the material which you are researching. It is likely that the amount of material which you will draw together for each area of work will seem to be daunting. At this stage it will be necessary to try to classify and sequence. This will be achieved by putting together aspects of the theme/topic into a small number of broad areas, perhaps thinking about them as weekly themes within the totality. The sequence in which you place the activities will be influenced by such factors as coherence for the children, their likely enthusiasm, access to resources as well as your own degree of confidence with the material.

At the end of this first stage you should have a resource of material for the different areas summarised into a flow chart which indicates its relationship with identified National Curriculum requirements. Within the flow chart or separately the ideas/ activities and a sequence for their presentation to the children will be indicated.

Stage 2: Building ideas into plans

At this stage you will need to look closely at each curriculum area which the theme/topic is intended to address. Working from the flow chart you will consider the key concepts in each curriculum area which have been identified for this class in the long-term planning and relate them to the chosen theme/topic, establishing broad aims for yourself. Then you will need to think in detail about what understandings and skills you want the children to acquire, i.e. you will establish your intentions for the children's learning.

The next stage will be to consider exactly what learning processes the children will be involved in, e.g. whether the children will be observing, hypothesising, testing, etc. Whatever activities they will be engaged in will have implications for the sequencing of the material, the response to individual needs, the teaching/learning approach adopted and the methods which will be used for assessment. All of these will receive attention in later chapters. The task now is to try to show how this might be effected using the example above.

The ideas outlined above are not easy to follow without a context within which they may be placed. A case study is available in Section 1, pp. 61–6 which may help. It refers to a topic on 'the school in the community' and focuses on the curriculum areas of Geography, History and Technology. As well as the work associated with the school itself the classteacher has seen the potential of a local community situation: the misuse of the open, grassed area in front of a residential home for the elderly adjacent to the school.

This case study:

• explores the school context
• sets out a flow chart
• follows this up with a possible sequence through the topic
• sets out stage 2 planning for the technology aspect of the topic and the cross-curricular theme of 'Citizenship'.

Using the stage 1 material from the case study (pp. 63–4), the next section will apply the model of medium-term planning to the historical aspect of the topic.

USING THE MEDIUM-TERM MODEL TO PLAN FOR HISTORY

According to the school's long-term plans, this class should be using a local study unit to explore the aspects of History. Using this as a basis the general aims may be:

• For the children to recognise, describe and give reasons for changes over a period of time
• For the children to make deductions from historical sources

A record of the brainstorming and 'sequence through the theme' is available in stage

1 of the case study and shows a number of activities related to these aims which may be developed, including the following.

Observing the building:

- looking for cues
- using worksheets and then children's own questions
- diagrams to show the 'old' and the 'new'
- observational drawings – charcoal, pencil

Interrogating resources:

- research into building styles
- using the school log and headteacher's diary
- 'how schools used to be', visit to local museum
- oral history – grandparent to visit school (one who lives in sheltered housing at the Wheatfields)

The first action at stage 2 is to state the intentions for learning and the associated learning experiences. For example, referring to 'looking for cues' a learning intention and the associated learning experiences might be:

- the children will recognise features in the school which associate the building with certain periods of time and some associated learning experiences
- discuss with the children what is a historical 'clue'
- using a prepared worksheet send groups of children round identified areas of the school to search for and record 'clues'
- groups to share ideas with each other

Similar intentions for learning and associated activities may be planned for the other aspects of 'observing the building' and for 'interrogating resources'. This planning will constitute stage 2(i).

The next step (stage 2(ii)) will be to identify the skills and processes of learning which will underlie these activities. Again, these are summarised in the flow chart in the case study (p. 63), i.e. raising questions, observing, analysing, presenting information, etc. Stage 2(iii) requires you to think carefully about sequencing the activities. The general sequence through the topic has already been considered in the first stage of the case study, but you will want to think about the sequence through the History section and what is the best order in which the activities may be undertaken by the children. For example, is it better for them to learn about evidence and historical background and then explore their own environment or to explore the school and then locate their findings in a more historical context? These decisions will be made on the basis of your knowledge of the children's interests and capabilities as well as your access to resources. All of this information may be recorded on a sheet like the one in Figure 3.4 and this will then provide the framework for your day-by-day planning.

The NCC guidelines anticipate that blocked units will be focused on a limited

TITLE OF UNIT		NC EXPECTATIONS		
OVERALL AIM(S)		CROSS-CURRICULAR ELEMENTS		
. . . .		. . . .		
Knowledge and understanding, skills, attitudes, processes of learning	*Session 1*	*Session 2*	*Session 3*	*Session 4*
Resources to be used		Assessment (overall mode)		

Figure 3.4 Form for recording a series of lessons' objectives and requirements

range of levels. However, it will be your responsibility to differentiate where this is necessary. For example, children with reading difficulties will need help when accessing written historical sources, especially where the writing is heavy or smudged. At this next stage (stage 2(iv)) you will be thinking about provision which will have to be made for individual children or groups.

Your plans will also need to consider teaching/learning approaches and assessment procedures. Both of these will be covered in later chapters so that at this point it is necessary, only, to raise them as important issues. Similar procedures will now need to be carried out for other aspects of your planning.

PLANNING FOR CROSS-CURRICULAR LINKS

We have already discussed how certain curriculum areas may be associated with one another within a single topic, e.g. Geography, History and Technology in the example above. The NCC guidelines stress that this should happen only if it does not threaten the character and identity of the subject or subjects concerned. It is clear that sensible links can also enhance children's learning and any teacher will take advantage of such possibilities.

The extended case-study example in Section 1 on pp. 65–6 shows two further examples of this:

- reinforcement of children's skills in English, i.e. writing letters, locating addresses, etc.
- the introduction of concepts from cross-curricular themes (see Section 1, p. 65)

PLANNING FOR CONTINUING UNITS

We have already suggested that the principles of planning apply generally to development of different units of work. However, it will be helpful to highlight the similarities and differences in planning blocked units (see the example for History above) and continuing units.

Take, for example, an aspect of the continuing unit in Maths which was identified for the class above: application of number skills in solving problems.

At stage 1(i) you would consider the progress of the children at this point in order to decide whether you are reinforcing skills which have been successfully developed or whether this is an area of weakness of this class. This assessment will influence the approach which you will decide to take.

At stages 1(ii)/(iii)/(iv) you will research the area very thoroughly, identifying all the skills which could be explored with the children and some of the activities which would interest and enthuse them as well as developing your own understanding of the problem-solving process. The latter will be very important because it is only by recognising the small steps which make up the problem-solving process that you will be able to break down the skills into the small steps which some of the children will require. Sequencing is another very important aspect of the building up of skills and your outcome at the end of stage 1 will show the detail of your breakdown of the skills and the sequence in which they will need to be presented to the children. You will also have identified the links which may be made with other work which you will be undertaking that term. An important factor in problem solving is practice in different situations and the topic(s) you a re-covering may offer that important opportunity. The stage 2 planning in the case study indicates some useful possibilities.

In considering stage 2(i) you will now set out your intentions for the children's learning related to this area of work. Using the outcomes of your research at stage 1 you will decide which skills the children will be able to tackle at this point in time.

At stages 2(ii) and 2(iii) you will again make use of your research at stage 1 to set out formally in sequence the processes which the children will need to undertake to achieve success.

Stage 2(iv) will have to be tackled in a very thorough way since for each child you will need to assess where they are located in the sequence of skills which you have identified. It is very likely that you will need to group the children according to what they have already achieved. The teaching/learning approach which you decide to adopt *at stage 2(v)* will relate to that assessment and subsequent grouping.

The precise way in which you will track children's developing skills will be your task for *stage 2(vi)*.

CONCLUSION

The processes of planning described in this chapter may seem difficult to follow and laborious. However, like driving a car, they get easier with practice. Each step which is dealt with systematically makes the next step easier. Careful and thorough planning is the basis for effective teaching and hard work in those early stages reaps great benefits later.

The National Curriculum shown in diagrammatic form

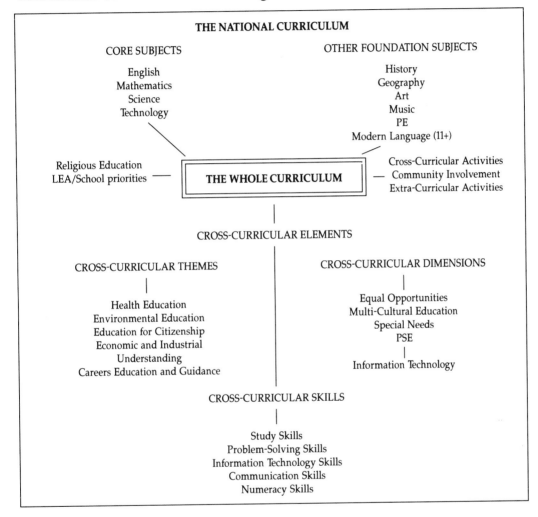

An example of medium-term planning

The following is a case study of the form of planning which has been explored in this chapter. It illustrates one form of planning which may form a model to be adapted to suit the purposes of different individuals or schools.

Issues for consideration are:

- Does this form of planning offer enough subject differentiation?
- Is this the most effective way of delivering cross-curriculum themes?

This example sets out the two stages in medium-term planning.

The context

The classteacher has identified 'the school within the community' as the theme for the term. The focus in the first half-term will be the school itself, which has an old part of the building dating from 1897. The teacher is anxious to develop the children's awareness of continuity and change, initially through active experience of looking at the old building, noting similarities and differences. She is also keen to develop the children's mapping and locational skills, at levels suited to the differing levels of ability within the class. The major curriculum focus will be history and geography.

As the student-teacher and the classteacher talk, it becomes apparent that the intentions for learning must go beyond these historical concepts and geographical skills. As activities are discussed, the student and mentor together begin to identify the *processes* that the children would be going through as they work. For example, in looking at the provision for access to the building, the children will have to observe, collect data upon and describe the existing situation; they must learn the opinions of all users of the building as to suggestions for improving provision, which involves questioning, devising interview schedules, listening, recording and interpreting.

The *cross-curricular dimensions* of Equal Opportunity and Personal and Social Education are also seen by both student and mentor as very evident strands within this topic; that will need to be recorded in the planning.

The cross-curricular dimension of *Citizenship* was also identified as an aspect that would be covered in the second half-term. The class teacher has seen the potential of a local community situation: the misuse of the open, grassed area in front of the residential home for the elderly adjacent to school. As they talk, the student suggests the final phase of the theme – designing and making a sign.

Stage 1 planning is therefore shown in this example as:

- a 'tidied-up' flow-chart showing the initial ideas reorganised into broad curriculum areas with linked boxes to indicate processes of learning
- the planned-for progression through the topic

Stage 2 planning shown here focuses upon the third and final phase, the sign for the residential home. The curriculum area is designated as Technology, the cross-curricular theme as Citizenship. However, the learning experiences planned allows for the development of the cross-curricular skills of communication, numerary, oracy, literacy, study skills and problem solving. The range of task demand within the activities also allowed the student, with the help of the teacher, to present appropriate tasks to individuals and groups of children within the class.

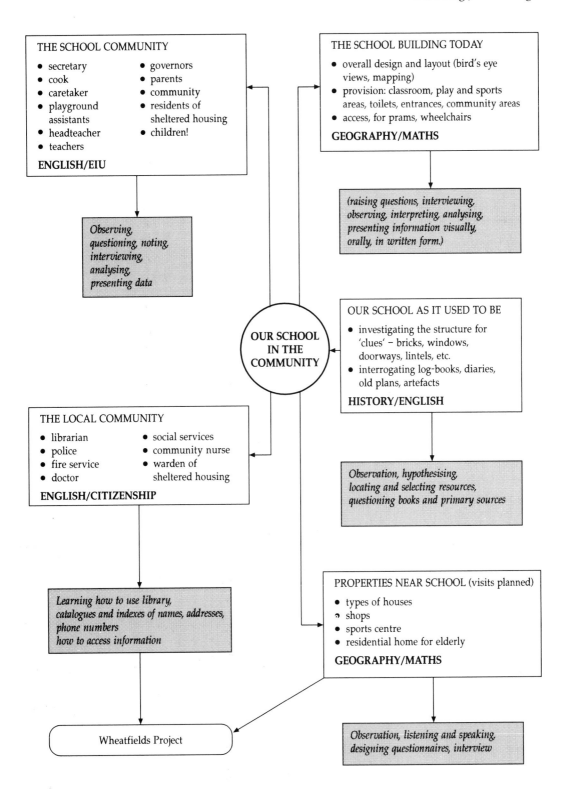

THE SCHOOL COMMUNITY
- secretary
- cook
- caretaker
- playground assistants
- headteacher
- teachers
- governors
- parents
- community
- residents of sheltered housing
- children!

ENGLISH/EIU

Observing, questioning, noting, interviewing, analysing, presenting data

THE SCHOOL BUILDING TODAY
- overall design and layout (bird's eye views, mapping)
- provision: classroom, play and sports areas, toilets, entrances, community areas
- access, for prams, wheelchairs

GEOGRAPHY/MATHS

(raising questions, interviewing, observing, interpreting, analysing, presenting information visually, orally, in written form.)

OUR SCHOOL IN THE COMMUNITY

OUR SCHOOL AS IT USED TO BE
- investigating the structure for 'clues' – bricks, windows, doorways, lintels, etc.
- interrogating log-books, diaries, old plans, artefacts

HISTORY/ENGLISH

Observation, hypothesising, locating and selecting resources, questioning books and primary sources

THE LOCAL COMMUNITY
- librarian
- police
- fire service
- doctor
- social services
- community nurse
- warden of sheltered housing

ENGLISH/CITIZENSHIP

Learning how to use library, catalogues and indexes of names, addresses, phone numbers how to access information

PROPERTIES NEAR SCHOOL (visits planned)
- types of houses
- shops
- sports centre
- residential home for elderly

GEOGRAPHY/MATHS

Wheatfields Project

Observation, listening and speaking, designing questionnaires, interview

SEQUENCE THROUGH THE TOPIC

THE SCHOOL BUILDING TODAY ACTIVITIES

Mapping (Geog)
- plans of school – bird's eye view, scale maps
- routes to school
- location of school within the local area

Provision/Access (citizenship, equal opps, pse)
- OBSERVATION schedules
- questionnaires
- charts and diagrams to suggest improvements
- presentation of main findings

THE SCHOOL IN THE PAST ACTIVITIES

Observing the building (History local study unit)
- looking for clues – using worksheet and then children's own questions
- diagrams to show the 'old' and the 'new'
- observational drawing – charcoal/pencil

Interrogating resources
- research into building styles
- using the school log and HTs diary
- 'how schools used to be': visit to Wigan Pier and follow-up work
- oral history – grandparent to visit school (who lives in sheltered housing 'Wheatfields')

Designing and making a sign for the front of 'Wheatfields'
(Technology, English, Citizenship)

STAGE 2   PLANNING: TECHNOLOGY/CITIZENSHIP

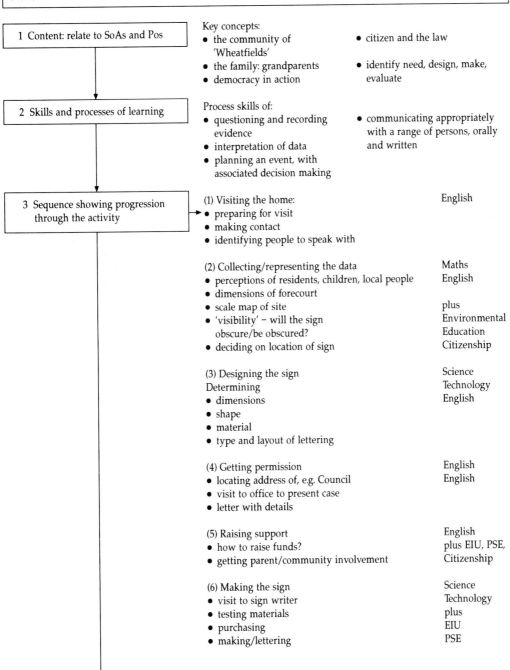

1 Content: relate to SoAs and Pos	Key concepts:	
	• the community of 'Wheatfields'	• citizen and the law
	• the family: grandparents	• identify need, design, make, evaluate
	• democracy in action	

2 Skills and processes of learning	Process skills of:	
	• questioning and recording evidence	• communicating appropriately with a range of persons, orally and written
	• interpretation of data	
	• planning an event, with associated decision making	

3 Sequence showing progression through the activity	(1) Visiting the home:	English
	• preparing for visit	
	• making contact	
	• identifying people to speak with	
	(2) Collecting/representing the data	Maths
	• perceptions of residents, children, local people	English
	• dimensions of forecourt	
	• scale map of site	plus
	• 'visibility' – will the sign obscure/be obscured?	Environmental Education
	• deciding on location of sign	Citizenship
	(3) Designing the sign	Science
	Determining	Technology
	• dimensions	English
	• shape	
	• material	
	• type and layout of lettering	
	(4) Getting permission	English
	• locating address of, e.g. Council	English
	• visit to office to present case	
	• letter with details	
	(5) Raising support	English
	• how to raise funds?	plus EIU, PSE,
	• getting parent/community involvement	Citizenship
	(6) Making the sign	Science
	• visit to sign writer	Technology
	• testing materials	plus
	• purchasing	EIU
	• making/lettering	PSE

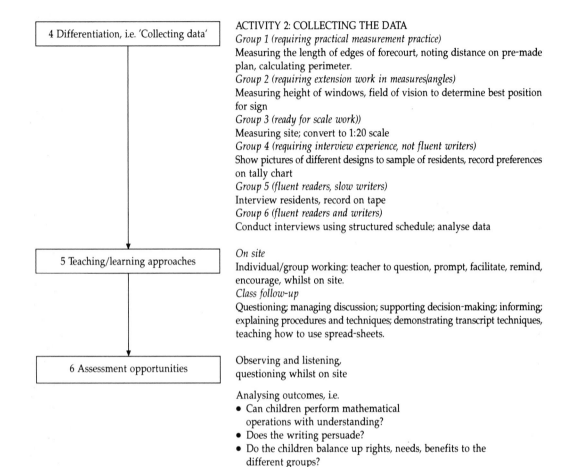

| 4 Differentiation, i.e. 'Collecting data' | ACTIVITY 2: COLLECTING THE DATA |

ACTIVITY 2: COLLECTING THE DATA
Group 1 (requiring practical measurement practice)
Measuring the length of edges of forecourt, noting distance on pre-made plan, calculating perimeter.
Group 2 (requiring extension work in measures/angles)
Measuring height of windows, field of vision to determine best position for sign
Group 3 (ready for scale work))
Measuring site; convert to 1:20 scale
Group 4 (requiring interview experience, not fluent writers)
Show pictures of different designs to sample of residents, record preferences on tally chart
Group 5 (fluent readers, slow writers)
Interview residents, record on tape
Group 6 (fluent readers and writers)
Conduct interviews using structured schedule; analyse data

5 Teaching/learning approaches

On site
Individual/group working: teacher to question, prompt, facilitate, remind, encourage, whilst on site.
Class follow-up
Questioning; managing discussion; supporting decision-making; informing; explaining procedures and techniques; demonstrating transcript techniques, teaching how to use spread-sheets.

6 Assessment opportunities

Observing and listening, questioning whilst on site

Analysing outcomes, i.e.
- Can children perform mathematical operations with understanding?
- Does the writing persuade?
- Do the children balance up rights, needs, benefits to the different groups?

Thematic and Subject Teaching

An issue which has been occupying educationalists at the present time is the potential conflict between presenting curriculum material in a way which is meaningful to children but which also allows for the maintenance of the 'identity and particular character of each subject'.

The arguments for an integrated curriculum

- It accords with the way children view the world.
- The 'whole personality' is best served by a holistic approach to the curriculum.
- It opens channels of investigation which subject specialist curriculum boundaries may close.

- It facilitates a rhythm of learning so that individual rates and types of learning are not strangled by constantly switching subjects.
- Children are given power to pursue their own learning paths.
- In a subject curriculum knowledge is unfairly represented as discrete packages; the key concepts which straddle subject boundaries are not given their proper place.

For a more detailed discussion see Morrison and Ridley (1988).

The arguments for a subject-based curriculum

- Subjects have identity and characteristics which children should be enabled to identify.
- It is argued that thematic teaching has not been carried out in a rigorous manner.
- In thematic teaching areas of the curriculum are not addressed.
- By using a subject-based approach schools will be better able to ensure that all aspects of the curriculum are given an appropriate allocation of time and resources.
- Subject teaching will allow for the better use of subject specialists to enhance teaching.

For more detailed discussion see:

NCC (1993) *Planning the National Curriculum at Key Stage 2*
OFSTED (1993) *Curriculum Organisation and Classroom Practice in Primary Schools: a follow-up report*

With an understanding of the issues involved teachers will be able to decide on a teaching approach which will reconcile the two approaches.

National curriculum guidance on planning

In the booklet *Planning the National Curriculum at Key Stage 2*, the National Curriculum Council sets out quite prescriptive guidelines for curriculum planning. The guidance is based on some detailed trials with schools and the suggestion is that although the focus is on Key Stage 2, 'it should provide a good basis for planning at Key Stage'. The foreword goes on to state that: 'In that it describes an approach to planning which can be applied to any curriculum content, it will not be affected by any future changes which might be made to the National Curriculum.'
  It identifies the following phases:

- Planning phase   Construct long-term plan for the whole key stage
  Develop medium-term plans for each class

- Implementation phase   Interim reviews (termly) enable individual teachers to modify (where necessary) their medium term plans

- Review phase   Review of long-term plan (annual) enables school to modify (where necessary) the long term plan

---

SECTION 2: ACTIVITIES

Activity 1

Using one of the formats for lesson planning described in the chapter, you and the classteacher write out a lesson plan, individually, for a session which will be carried out with the class. Share the plans with each other, noticing particularly where you have given emphasis to different things. Discuss these together.

Now read:
Berliner, D.C. and Carter, K.J. (1989) 'Differences in processing classroom information by expert and novice teachers', in J. Lowyck and C.M. Clark, *Teacher Thinking and Professional Action*, Leuven, Leuven University Press.
   Compare your discussions with their findings.

Activity 2

Re-read the paragraph 'Developing intentions for children's learning'. Now, thinking about the nature area in the school grounds and the two aims.

- 1b Observing and talking about a familiar place
- 2a Naming familiar features of the local area

Write two intentions for learning in a Y1 class related to the above. Be sure that the intention could form an objective for a particular teaching session.
   Now try the same exercise for a Y4 class related to an alternative National Curriculum requirement for Geography.

Activity 3

Re-read:

- a model for medium-term planning
- using the medium-term model to plan for History

Now using the case-study material on pp. 61–6 complete the planning exercise for History begun in the chapter.

Activity 4

Using the model for medium-term planning, plan for a continuing unit in order to enable the children in a Y1 class to: demonstrate knowledge of the alphabet in using wordbooks and simple dictionaries.

BIBLIOGRAPHY

Booth, T., Swann, W., Masterton, M. and Potts, P. (1991) *Curricula for Diversity in Education*, Routledge.
A book which looks at ways of including diversity in different areas of the curriculum.
Bourne, J. (1993) *Thinking Through Primary Practice*, Routledge.
A consideration of the primary curriculum in the light of debates about 'good practice'.
Curtis, A.M. (1986) *A Curriculum for the Pre-School Child*, Routledge.
A book which lays down a curriculum framework for three- to five-year-old children and the competencies and skills which should be fostered at this time.
Fyfe, A. and Figueroa, P. (1993) *Education for Cultural Diversity*, Routledge.
A book which relates the curriculum to a 'positive, proactive approach to education in a multi-cultural society'.
Lewis, A. (1991) *Primary Special Needs and the National Curriculum*, Routledge.
An analysis of ways in which the National Curriculum may be made available to children who find school-based learning difficult.
McNamara, D. (1993) *Classroom Pedagogy and Classroom Practice*, Routledge.
A book which defines the professional expertise of primary teachers and addresses some of the issues associated with the debates about teaching methods.
Morrison, K. and Ridley, K. (1988) *Curriculum Planning and the Primary School*, Paul Chapman Publishing Ltd.
This book looks at curriculum theory and its application to planning in primary schools. It addresses many of the issues and debates which concern primary teachers in a very accessible way.
National Curriculum Council (1993) *Planning The National Curriculum At Key Stage 2*, NCC.
A re-thinking of ways in which the National Curriculum may be delivered in primary schools. The recommendations are based on extensive discussions with primary school teachers. Although relating directly to Key Stage 2, it is seen to provide a 'good basis for planning at Key Stage 1' as well.
Office for Standards in Education (1993) *Curriculum Organisation and Classroom Practice in Primary Schools: a Follow-up Report*, OFSTED.
This report addresses itself directly to some of the issues of Subject versus Thematic planning as well as the associated teaching strategies.
Palmer, J. and Pettitt, D. (1993) *Topic Work in the Early Years*, Routledge.
A careful consideration of the use of topic work as a means of delivering the National Curriculum to young children.

Sweetmann, J. (1992) *Curriculum Confidential Three,* Bracken Press.
   A very readable book which puts into perspective some of the changes which have been made to the National Curriculum.

The National Curriculum Council produces many documents relating to the curriculum. Some of these are informational and others reflective of good practice. Information about these publications may be obtained from:
The School Curriculum and Assessment Authority
Customer Services Section, Newcombe House, 45 Notting Hill Gate, London W11 3JB.

4 TEACHING

In this chapter you will:

- learn about the present debate surrounding different teaching approaches;

- explore the elements of different modes or ways of teaching;

- see how your choice of teaching strategy must relate to your 'intentions for learning', and how the teacher's intervention affects the nature of the learning experience;

- identify and practice the particular features of teaching techniques;

- explore how a considered and innovative use of resources can enhance your teaching effectiveness.

To create an effective learning environment in which children feel 'brave' as described in Chapter 2, the teacher must be *very* skilful: able to understand the children as learners; know about and understand the National Curriculum; and be able to select smoothly from a range of teaching strategies. Part of the fascination and challenge of teaching as a profession is its complexity, which student-teachers in their first term of a teacher education course recognise and acknowledge.

' I realise now that teaching is a complex process'
'There is a lot more to it than I originally thought'
'Teaching is like driving a car: you have to think of many things all at once'

and

'There is not one "good" way to teach'

This last statement is especially relevant to teachers in training at the present time. The assumption that we all know what 'good' teaching is and and that it is instantly recognisable has recently been strongly challenged, with significant implications for teacher training. For this reason we devote a brief space in this chapter to certain key events and reports of the early 1990s.

The Report of the Evaluation Team of the Primary Needs Project in Leeds

(Alexander, 1991, published August, see Section 1, p. 102 for details) questioned the assertion that there is one model of 'good practice'. It also fuelled a lively debate about teaching methods. The report indicated the unease felt by the classroom teachers involved in the Leeds Project with what were described as 'multi-curriculum-focus' lessons, i.e. children working in small groups on a range of different activities. It was swiftly followed by an investigation called for by the DFE into the delivery of education in primary schools in England and Wales. The resulting DFE discussion paper 'Curriculum Organisation and Curriculum Practice in Primary Schools' was published in 1992 (DES 1992), followed in 1993 by a follow-up report from OFSTED (1993a), as well as other commentaries and critiques. (See Section 1, pp. 102–4 for fuller details of these and subsequent reports.)

Both the above recommend, amongst other things, a balance of whole class, group and individual teaching, and the deployment of a wide range of teaching techniques, according to the criteria of 'fitness for purpose'. These and other HMI/OFSTED reports indicated in Section 1 repay careful reading, as they contain much rich material about the skills and techniques of primary teaching.

Overall they reinforce what most primary teachers have always known: that a mix of methods makes for effective classroom practice. The mixture works best in classrooms where *children* are:

- clear about what they are doing and why they are doing it
- clear about what is expected of them in terms of quality and quantity of work completed
- confident that their learning efforts will be properly supported, their questions answered and difficulties dealt with

and in classrooms where the *teachers*:

- convey their appropriately high expectations for achievement and behaviour to their pupils

None of this makes learning how to teach any more straightforward, of course. There is no single recipe for successful teaching – it is a matter of making wise choices, from an available range of teaching and organisational competencies, to suit your particular purpose. But don't feel daunted. This chapter will help you to learn about some of the necessary teaching skills and strategies, and suggest ways in which you might try them out in practice.

WAYS OF TEACHING

So far, we have used terms interchangeably – 'teaching approaches', 'teaching strategies', 'teaching skills', 'teaching methods' – as you will find to be the case in much of the literature of pedagogy. It will be useful prior to reading the rest of this chapter to attempt to sort out these terms. Figure 4.1 is an attempt to show you how we define

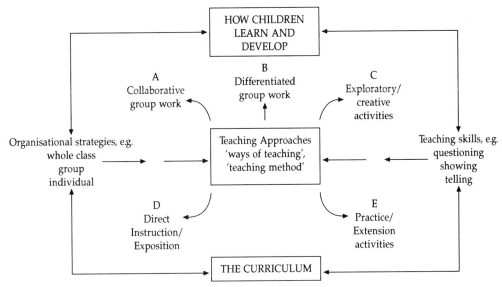

Figure 4.1 Teaching approaches

'Teaching Approaches' in relation to an overall model of teaching and learning in primary classrooms.

The various terms in the central box of Figure 4.1 – 'teaching approaches', 'ways of teaching', 'teaching method' – are used as generic labels for the same thing – the broad professional practices that primary school teachers select from and use. We will examine these in detail later in the chapter. You can see by looking at the Teaching Approaches 'web' that we use the term 'Teaching Approach' to describe decisions made by the teacher about the *nature* of the learning experience to be engaged in by the children. From the position of the box, you can see that the choice of an approach is influenced by three significant strands in primary school education:

- how *children* learn and develop
- the *curriculum* to be delivered
- the *teacher's* choice of organisational and teaching strategies

If we look at the interplay between the three parallel 'teacher' boxes in the diagram, we see that Organisational Strategies and Teaching Skills feed into the Teaching Approaches box, but remain apart, *to be selected from as appropriate*. This is an important point: don't make the mistake of thinking that the choice of a teaching approach, e.g. collaborative group working or direct instruction/exposition relies upon one set of closely related and discrete teaching skills. This is most definitely not the case, and choices about when, how and indeed whether to 'explain things', or 'demonstrate' or 'question' are open to you as you work within *any* approach, whether it be with a small group, individuals or a full class. High-level teacher interaction, with teaching targeted at specific pupils or groups, should be a part of any method. The 'teacher's role' column on our lesson plan format allows you to show how you plan for such purposeful intervention.

This *focused teaching* may be pre-determined and shown in your plan or it may emerge from careful observation and monitoring of the pupils at work. An example will show how vital a skill this is.

Example: Design/Technology, Year 6

Martin is on his first school placement. In a previous lesson he had already given the children a design brief: work in pairs to construct an item for an Adventure Playground from paper and card.

At the start of the second lesson his learning intentions were:

- for the children to complete their design already begun
- for the children to translate the design into a model

Resources

He had prepared his resources very carefully, having available pieces of card cut to various sizes, scissors, etc.

How he began

Martin introduced the session quite briefly through refocusing the children on a diagrammatic representation of the design process. He then asked the children to begin work, whilst he and his student-teacher partner moved between the children, advising, monitoring, helping with tricky bits of cutting and sticking, chivvying slower workers, etc.

To intervene or not intervene?

He noticed after about twenty minutes that the most successful pairs were those who had carefully labelled each part of their design with the material or resources from which it would be made. However, as Martin was still not confident that he could get the attention of the children readily, and as they all appeared to be 'getting on', he decided to spread this news on a one-to-one basis rather than demonstrate to the class as a whole the good work of the achieving pupils.

What he did

So many children needed help with the manipulative aspects that he was not able to return to the struggling designers, who had still not had any success with building a model by playtime.

What he wished he had done

Martin wished that he had stopped all the class and shared with them the detailed, labelled designs and emergent models to reinforce his teaching points about the design process. If Martin had done as he wished,with a re-focusing of the children on the task by re-explaining and emphasising, his learning intentions would have been more fully achieved – a missed opportunity to practice *focused teaching*.

TEACHING APPROACHES

Each approach contains certain features or *elements* that determine what it is that the teacher must do, encourage or sustain in order to use the approach effectively.

Collaborative group work

The children are required to work together in a group in which members are at different levels of ability and achievement. The group is to produce a *shared outcome* and so the critical feature for the teacher is to identify the right sort of task. It is no good asking children to work collaboratively together as a group if the activity invites a large amount of independent working, with the possibility of individual outcomes! Similarly, there must be opportunities for individual children to contribute at their own individual level of skill and understanding. Consider this example.

Example: English, Year 6: 'Zoo Leaflet'

The children have been on a visit to the zoo. Student-teachers Rupinder and Jeannie ask each group of six children to produce a joint 'visitors' leaflet' about all the animals they have seen, containing information about their natural habitats, life-cycle, etc. Single sheets of lined A4 paper are provided with no suggestion as to the final appearance of the leaflet – size, shape – nor whom the audience is to be. The children decide to work in pairs, each choosing an animal, and proceed to draw and write on both sides of the paper, which they fold in assorted ways. At the end of the session there are three drawings of a panda with short descriptions of its appearance, and one giraffe has been described. They have no ideas about how to collate all their information into a presentable leaflet.

On reflection Jeannie and Rupinder realised that for the children to work together on the task they should have done certain things germane to the *elements* of collaborative working. They should have:

- made the goal for the group clear. This could have been done by showing the children a ready-made up booklet in which the information could be displayed. Element: *defining the activity*. Children need to understand the task through seeing the sort of outcome that is expected of them.

- suggested that the cover, overall design features, list of contents, factual information, illustrations, etc. be the known responsibility of certain group members. Element: *helping children's understanding of roles and responsibilities*. The pupils should be able to share out tasks between individuals within the group.

- allocated the children time to discuss what kind of an activity this was to be and what they would be involved in as a group. Element: *task orientation*. Time for this stage within a collaborative task is often insufficient. Once the task has been explained in terms of outcomes and roles, participants in a group working situation need time to talk around the task, to explore together as a group the sorts of activities and decisions they will be making in the process of their collaborative efforts.

- prepared a set of differently coloured and sized paper, with instructions that the group had to decide upon uniformity of colour and size. Element: *ensuring joint decision-making*. By thoughtful, limited provision of resources the teacher can force the children's hand, denying them the possibility of individual rather than collaborative responses.

- directed the children to the information books by inserting cue-cards containing open and focused questions at appropriate pages. Element: *awareness of prerequisite skills*. The teacher must identify the level of skill and understanding required for the task and match it to the children in the group. In this way she or he can prevent any lack of skill from debarring certain group members from making a contribution.

Differentiated group work

There are two possible situations stemming from this example which could operate as differentiated group work. First, as in the zoo example above, the children will probably be required to produce a joint, group outcome. In this case, though, the group will be at a *similar* level of skill development and will all make a *similar* level and type of contribution. In the example above, each child would have contributed an animal –

picture, description and information selected from reference texts. Second, there may be a situation where the teacher has identified a group of children who share a particular problem, are ready to learn the next step in a learning sequence, or are possibly in need of extending and challenging experiences in a particular way. Again to take the zoo example, the need might be to introduce or reinforce information retrieval skills – use of index, contents page, skimming and scanning, etc. The significant feature is that the task will be matched to the needs of this particular set of learners.

The elements of both these group situations are similar. The children will need:

- a clear explanation of the task before them
  Element: *defining the activity* as shown above.

- a level of knowledge of the skills or understandings required with an opportunity of 'learning about' or practising these with the teacher first of all, before engaging with the task
  Element: *prerequisite skills to be developed.* In this case, the teacher intends to teach the children something new, rather than facilitate the use of previously acquired or partially acquired skills.

- time to talk together to explore the task's demands and make decisions, in these examples about who 'does' which animal, format of the work, etc.
  Element: *roles and responsibilities/task orientation.* Time for this stage is as important here as in collaborative working.

- an accessible supply of appropriate resources
  Element: *match of materials to task* and task to levels of attainment of the group members.

Exploratory group activity

Exploratory activity has many of the same elements as the teaching approach shown above:

- the children need to be clear about what they are to do and why
  Element: *defining the nature of activity*

- the children need a certain level of skill development or knowledge base
  Element: *prerequisite skill development*

- the children must all feel they can and should make a contribution
  Element: *understanding of roles*

This type of group work also requires that:

- the group need to feel that their ideas and opinions are valued
  Element: *creating an appropriate climate*

- talk must be seen as a valued part of the activity
  Element: *function of conversation*

- the children must have opportunity to play with, handle, experiment with, try out, and examine materials, artefacts and resources
  Element: *process orientation rather than product.* The teacher must show the children that their talk, actions and working procedures are as valuable as the final product.

Direct Instruction/Exposition

This teaching approach involves relaying to the children information which you hold that they don't – perhaps about an event or object (say the London Blitz or a thermometer), or a particular skill, say loading a floppy disk or playing a guitar chord. Here is an example of an exposition in the curriculum area of Mathematics, illustrated using lesson plan headings to help you see the link between Planning and Teaching Approach.

Example: Mathematics, Year 6: 'Coordinates'

Joanne intends to teach a Year 6 class how to set out and use a locational grid, with two-figure coordinates. From the previous day's work, she has seen that many children are not able to properly label the axes and are confused as to how to read off the points on the grid. This is how she explained and instructed the children, using an Exposition/Direct Instruction approach (see Plan 4.1).

   We can unpack this example in order to see the elements of which it is composed, which match the numbered stages on the plan. You may elaborate upon these for yourself with the help of the plan. Elements of the exposition are:

- the attractively produced map (1)
  Element: *getting attention*

- careful introduction of mathematical terms, e.g. axis (7, 8)
  Element: *controlled, systematic use of technical language*

- questions about what the children can see/know (2, 5, 6, etc.)
  Element: *building upon existing knowledge or understanding*

- visual reinforcement of key words (8, 12)
  Element: *reinforcement and alternative representation*

- steady progression from one point to the next (13, 14, 15)
  Element: *clarity of sequence*

- division into small learning steps (16, 17)
  Element: *size of steps appropriate to task and learner needs*

Introduction	Points to remember
Settle the children in a semi-circle around me, with OHP and flip chart nearby	Check pens for OHP/flip chart
1 Show children ready-made colourful treasure map on OHP with island features	Point to treasure
2 Where is the treasure?	Allow range of answers
3 How could we tell somebody where the treasure is?	Listen to ideas; try to draw out idea of location
Development	
4 Overlay grid	
5 How does this help?	
6 What else do we need?	
7 What is this line called?	Check for use of word 'axis'
8 Write the word axis on the flip chart	Repeat 'axis' as it is written
9 What is this line called?	Run finger along and up, on map
10 How do we know which axis we are talking about?	
11 Tell them the names	Draw axis, write name along
12 Write the names on the flip chart	
13 Write the first number on the horizontal axis.	
14 Tell that must be 0	Write in 0
15 Where do we put the first number on the vertical axis?	
16 What number will this be?	Ask for responses from as many children as possible
17 Who can tell me the next number?	
18 and the next? and the next?	
19 So we have learned to go up one each time, and we put the number on the *line.*	Repeat several times, pointing to different numbers along the line
(DO SAME FOR BOTH AXES, inviting children to write and name.)	
20 What name shall we give the treasure?	
21 Does it matter which way we say the numbers?	
(*Try out the same point both ways*)	
22 We always write the horizontal first	Write down each pin-point both ways – point out difference in location
23 This is how we write it	Show how to use brackets and comma: (4,2)
24 What name would we give to a tree here?	Wait for most children to attempt to answer

Plan 4.1 Example of exposition/direct instruction approach

- opportunity to practice what has been learned (18, 19)
  Element: *giving practice, consolidation*

- asking questions about what has been learned (20)
  Element: *checking for understanding*

- the drawing together of what has been learned (19)
  Element: *use of summary to reassure, consolidate, support*

Notice how a range of teaching skills come into this particular Teaching Approach – explaining, questioning, demonstrating, reinforcing, practising. And so does decision making about organisational strategies, because although this was a class lesson, it could equally have been the teacher working with a small group who were ready for this work, as in the differentiated example above. You can see nicely from this how both teaching techniques and organisational strategies feed into the chosen Teaching Approach, contributing to a well-matched teaching session that shows 'fitness for purpose'.

Practice and extension tasks

Practice activity

Following the explanation, in the development stage of the lesson, Joanne gives the children a worksheet on which there is a different treasure map, overlaid by a grid numbered 0 to 12 on each axis. This is shown on her lesson plan under 'resources'. On the more detailed plan, she notes:

Worksheet: treasure map grid as in 'introduction' stage, containing two kinds of practice task involving two-figure coordinates. The questions ask the children to:

- locate and name items on the map through finding and reading off their position
- and, conversely, give grid references for certain named features.

Before asking the children to begin work she shows good understanding of the elements of a *practice* activity by:

- telling the children that this is an opportunity to practise coordinates, so that they know why they are doing the activity
  Element: *relationship to previous learning*

- quickly pointing out the two different kinds of task
  Element: *defining the nature of the activity*

- working out the first of each example type on the flip chart
  Element: *consolidating, reinforcing*

- showing how and where the answer is to be set down
  Element: *clarifying procedures*

- telling the children that the task should take them about half an hour
  Element: *setting appropriate expectations*

- asking them to work independently
  Element: *individual reinforcement and consolidation*

In this practice activity Joanne chose to keep the class working as a class, but she could have allowed some children to engage in other activities, e.g. computing, or exploratory tasks to maximise upon resources. Practice activities can be class, group or individually organised.

Extension activity

Joanne knew that certain children had understood the work before the lesson began, but in order to give her undivided attention to the majority who were in need of instruction or reinforcement, she decided to include them in the class exposition. However, at the follow-up stage, she differentiated the work for them, by supplying them with a different example of a map, with unmarked axes, a finer grid and more features. Their task was to locate the features and give each feature a grid reference; they also had to plot a route to the treasure, showing the grid references at significant direction points.

This activity contains all the elements of an extension activity, i.e. *reinforcement* of what has been learned through independent practice, and *application* of new learning to a similar but more complex situation. Joanne drew this group to one side; she did not 'go over' each question but (1) checked for understanding of numbering of axes, (2) reminded them of how to record two-figure coordinates and (3) identified a trickily positioned feature as posing a challenge.

SELECTING TEACHING APPROACHES

So how do you choose which Teaching Approach to adopt for a certain session, with appropriate organisational and teaching strategies to support and enrich your choice? The answer of course is that you choose ways of teaching that best fit your learning intentions, which you must set against the model of primary education that we saw at the start. Here is one example of what we mean.

Example: Science, Year 2

You have brought into school a collection of six snails which you want the children to observe and raise their own questions about, as preparation for planning their own investigation. The learning intentions of your lesson/activity plan are for the children to:

- observe the snails closely
- make a careful observational drawing of one of the snails
- compare and contrast the snails – shell markings, size, trails, movement
- as a group, write down the one question that they would most like to find the answer to

If you compare these objectives to the elements of each Teaching Approach as outlined above, you will see that the best match is with exploratory activities where the focus of such activity is in the children looking, talking, considering, examining, which is what you want to promote in this Science task.

This seems straightforward enough but other considerations come into play as you review possible organisational and teaching strategies.

Applying the model

You now need to apply our model of teaching and learning in primary classrooms, with its three strands, the child, the curriculum and the teacher. You will find this especially relevant as a student-teacher when you have to fit into the curriculum organisation and practice of schools and classrooms in which you are placed. Let us apply the model to the suggested approach of exploratory learning.

Expectations as learners: '"children as learners" factors'

You know from theories of how children learn that exploration and interaction are important for children of this age. You also know that you have to take the children's previous experiences as learners into account; and in this classroom, the children are often taught as a class, with much individual practice activities from workcards and worksheets. Group working has not been a frequent feature of their classroom learning, so you wish to accommodate to this.

The nature of the activity/task: 'curriculum factors'

Here, everything points in the direction of small-group working of an exploratory nature, as originally decided. The scientific skills of observation, comparison and question-raising are best developed through first-hand experience of living/real things – snails in this case – shared with others through exploratory talk. What is more, your resources for this scientific activity – six snails, four large magnifiers and six soft-lead pencils for observational drawing – reinforce this organisational choice of a small group.

Teaching techniques: 'teacher factors'

So how to solve the dilemma of introducing exploratory group activities to these children whilst seeing to the needs of the rest of the class, who are used to a considerable amount of teacher direction for their activities?

Teaching skills

It is now that you make a further selection. You need to find a way of *explaining* the task, *demonstrating* the skill of using the magnifier and *modelling* the raising of questions, as discussed below. You have to do this whilst keeping the rest of the children involved and on task.

A consideration of these factors may lead you to decide:

- Teaching Approach: exploratory accompanied by
- Organisation: whole class working plus a single working group engaged in science, accompanied by
- Teaching Strategy: explanation of both tasks made so interesting that all the class will listen and then be eager to hear about what the science group found out at the end of the session.

There are other ways in which your intentions for learning affect your choice of Teaching Approach and associated organisational and teaching strategies. The Zoo example showed the importance of planning for the learning needs of individuals and groups within the class and Joanne's lesson was an example of differentiating the follow-up activity to class-directed exposition. In the longer term Joanne would need to plan for this group separately, in order to properly match the task to ability/ attainment. She would therefore plan differentiated work for these children (as in differentiated work above), setting different objectives for the group.

In her planning and then in implementing her teaching she would:

- group children according to their abilities, so as to set appropriately demanding tasks
- purposefully move between activities to explain, instruct, question, assess
- plan her teacher time so as to give sufficient attention to the class, to groups and to individuals.

Such differentiation by task and its classroom management requires meticulous planning and even more meticulous classroom organisation as explored in the section that follows.

Organisational strategies

The organisational model that we refer to so far, of class, group or individual is deceptively simple as you will have realised from our examples and your own experience. Teachers not only opt for a balance between the three but, as we have seen, plan sessions in which there is an overlap between the three modes. Initially, you should aim to take or retain responsibility for the class whilst dealing with one or more groups. The number of groups can then rise as you get more proficient. Also, you need to be aware of how the structured intervention of the teacher can alter the level and mode of functioning of a group. The following is an example of this.

Example: Year 2: English session: small-group organisation

At the start of the morning Steve and Diane plan that four related activities will take place linked to the class theme of Ourselves, including the aspect of Growing Up (see Figure 4.2). The writing, reading and speaking/listening activities are differentiated to match the different abilities within the class and will be explained briefly to the class as a whole whilst they are seated round the teacher at the start of the morning.

Steve and Diane decide to think about each group in terms of the anticipated level of teacher input, terming these *H* (high), *M* (medium) and *L* (low) as outlined in Plan 4.2.

This means that following the initial introduction from 9.15 to 9.30, they can focus their teaching like this:

9.30 am   Start off science report group
9.40 am   Discuss 'all about me' booklet with writing group
9.45 am   Check role-play and puppets groups, listen to initial ideas

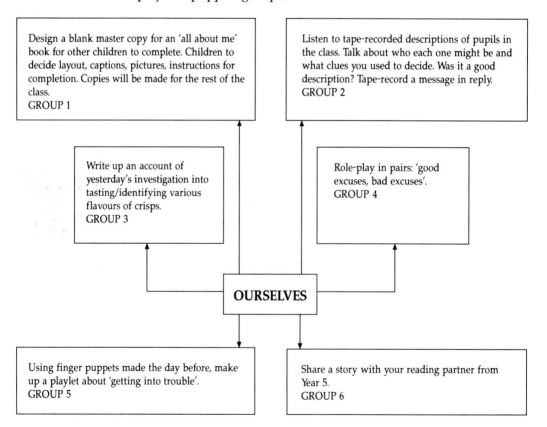

Figure 4.2 Organisation of group work

9.55 am   Read science reports, give feedback

10.10 am   Discuss plans for booklet with group, read/respond to examples completed.

10.20 am   Work with listeners to tape-recording. Ask questions to promote justifications for identifications made

10.30 am   Bring role-play and finger puppets together to share outcomes

L **Low** teacher input (using finger puppets, role play)	Listen and participate as group member, look for, suggest and teach about characterisation through dialogue.
M **Medium** teacher input (account of science investigation and listening to tape)	Question about previous investigations; order events on flip chart; write key heading for report on chart. Probing questions: which were effective descriptions? Why?
H **High** level of input ('all about me' book)	Show commercial baby book; explain how class book compares/may be different; elicit and clarify information to be included; initiate ideas on layout.

Plan 4.2 Example of a plan showing levels of teacher input

There are several interesting features of this organisational plan.

- Diane and Steve have targeted their teaching so as to give instruction, praise and feedback as often and appropriately as they can. They plan for return visits to the science report group and the 'all about me' booklet group, as well as building in a brief monitoring of the speaking and listening activities.

- The medium-level activity changes into a high-level activity as they join the tape-recording group, probing and extending learning through re-focusing questions and suggestions.

- By bringing two groups together at the end, the tape-recording children are given an audience for their work and the opportunity to share their expertise in constructing dialogue.

You will note how very important is the role of the teacher in this lesson. Diane and Steve's sharply *focused teaching* is instrumental to its smooth running and the quality of pupil learning.

    (Activity 1 in Section 2, pp. 104–5 gives a similar example for you try.)

Introductions

You will also have realised that the class *introduction* referred to above is a critical feature of Steve and Diane's session in order to establish necessary rules and routines.

They seated the children on the carpeted area to show them several examples of commercial baby books to enthuse them and give an idea of what it was they were aiming to achieve. Children who did the Science investigation the day before were invited to say what they had found, and an outline structure for the report was worked out and pinned up, with a 'useful words' word-bank displayed. Procedural matters were dealt with as each group was dispatched to their work-station.

Such introductions are far from being restricted to one particular organisational pattern or Teaching Approach; nor do they use a single teaching technique. Rather, they are a phase or stage in the lesson, in which the teachers will deploy a selection of teaching skills, i.e. explanation, instruction, questioning, checking, demonstrating. In an effective introduction these skills must be used flexibly and fluently to make sure that the children are clear about *what* they are meant to be doing, *why*, *when* and with *whom*. An introduction often combines explanation of content with instruction about organisational matters.

A good whole-class introduction as with Diane and Steve should:

- inform about curriculum content
- enthuse, and clarify the nature of the task
- instruct about organisational matters

Leaving the children

- still interested in the topic, not bored by listening
- keen to start
- knowing what to do.

Planning introductions

In planning introductions that achieve these aims and facilitate the smooth running of your particular form of organisation, you need to ask yourself certain 'Introduction Planning Questions' as shown in the 'Introduction Checklist' in Figure 4.3. These start from the pupil perspective, by asking what it is that the child would wish or need to know/know about, as shown in the left-hand column. The teacher column is a list of corresponding questions you might ask yourself as you plan your introduction. If, through thinking ahead in this way, you can help the children to feel confident about the tasks you set, then such pre-session preparation will be well worth the extra effort.

Once you have thought through these questions, you will be ready to incorporate explanations, demonstration, questioning, into your planned introduction. You will find that getting the sequence right is not easy and you always have to compromise between saying too much and too little. You have to enthuse and inform about content and inform and direct about management issues, all without losing the interest or attention of the children.

(See Activity 2, Section 2, p. 106 for an introduction practice task.)

PUPIL NEEDS/QUERIES ➔⟵ ⟶	INTRODUCTION PLANNING QUESTIONS
(What *pupils* need to know)	(What the *teacher* needs to ask him/herself)
What am I to do?	How will the children come to know about the nature of the task, what I expect overall?
Why am I doing this?	How can I help the children to make the connections between this task, previous work and the overall theme or progression within the subject?
How am I supposed to tackle it?	How much information do I want to give to the children, how much do I purposely withhold? And how will I explain this to them so that the children understand my motives?
Who will be doing this with me?	Will the whole class work together? If not, will I use friendship groups, or ability groups? Will the tasks be better done individually? If so, is talk important, or necessary?
Where shall I do the task?	Will I allow an element of choice, or shall I direct the work-stations? In either case, how will the children know about these aspects?
What things will I need in order to get on?	What resources are needed, where will they be, and how can I best ensure that the children can make sensible and full use of them? Will there be new instructions or will I be reminding about established routines and procedures?
When should I have accomplished something?	How long should I allow for this task? How can I give the children a sense of purpose about time? Shall I set deadlines, and if so, at which point(s) in the lesson? How can I enforce these?
What will happen to the outcomes?	How can I ensure that the children appreciate the intended audience and purpose for the work, and know what to do with it, and how will they get feedback?

Figure 4.3 An introduction checklist

TEACHING TECHNIQUES AND SKILLS

In this section, we explore more closely the specific teaching techniques of explaining, questioning, instructing, demonstrating and giving feedback. As we shall see, these are inter-dependent, but to help you acquire the skills, it is useful to try to separate out their elements.

Explaining things

The distinction between explanation and instruction is not a sharp one – there is overlap. Broadly speaking, an explanation helps children to 'see' or understand how and why something can or should be done, whilst instruction 'tells' them how to do it, when and in what manner. If we return to Diane and Steve's lesson we can see this more clearly.

In Steve and Diane's lesson, the introduction contained elements of explanation and instruction, and also questioning: *explanation* – was about the purpose, nature, possible lay-out and appearance of the booklet; *instruction* – was about materials to use, time available for the task, expectations about neatness, accuracy, etc. and also *questions* – were about the children's ideas, how they envisaged the completed booklet, and to check understanding.

Explanations come at various stages in a teaching session, and may be directed to individuals, groups or the whole class. They are not the special preserve of whole-class lessons; focused teaching with groups of children requires the ability to explain things just as does whole-class working. Whatever the situation, the elements of a good explanation remain the same. These are laid out in the following sections, to help you in planning out your explanations, which should be very carefully prepared. You saw the care with which Joanne had thought through her explanation of coordinates for example. If you know what you want to say and have decided upon the simplest and clearest way of saying it, then it is more likely that your explanation will have the necessary *clarity*.

Starting from what the children know

Try to relate what you say to the children's own experience and build on this to take them forward in their learning.

- Find out what they already know from the teacher, your mentor or by questioning the children. Remember this is only your starting point. You are going to tell the children something 'new', 'extra', 'different'; don't rely upon the children's existing knowledge to run your explanation for you!
- Show them how the new learning will fit into what they are already working upon, know about and are able to do. Share your learning intentions with the children. Say things like 'When you have learned to do this, we will be able to ...', 'This fits in here because ...', 'We're going to use what we learned yesterday now, to ...'.

Link it together (continuity)

- try to keep to the topic; don't digress into side issues and lose the thread
- aim for fluency: think about how to make one point link to the next and how you

will cue the children into shifts from one step to the next. Use verbal cues like 'so, that's how we do that section. Now then, let's think about the next little bit' will give the children a mental set that there is a change of gear, that the explanation has moved into another stage.

Keep it simple

The trick here is to make your explanation appear simple. It won't be simple in the planning, of course!

- avoid grammatically complex sentences
- use short sentences if you can
- explain any specialist terms
- use vocabulary that is within the experience of the children

Emphasise and reinforce

You should aim to *emphasise* your key points. Try to:

- repeat and re-word main ideas as above
- talk about and put key words on the chalkboard as you go along and *use them often* in your explanation
- have the children repeat them and use them back in responses to questions
- vary the tone of your voice, to make things sound interesting, significant, worth knowing
- point to and refer to your resources, e.g. artefacts, pictures, maps, as you talk

Be explicit

Say what you mean. Don't say, 'so I want you to label the diagram properly'. Say, 'Now, remember to draw faint lines to write the label word on, and use a ruler to draw *in pencil* the line to the exact edge of the part on the diagram you are labelling'.

Give examples

- Use multiple ways of explaining, i.e. pictures, diagrams, artefacts, maps, real things, making sure that they are large and clear enough for all the children to see.
- Refer to the illustrations in your explanation; don't just say: 'Here's a picture of a windmill' and then carry on without further reference to the windmill in the picture.

Use it, make it work for you. Say, perhaps, 'What do you notice about the shape of the sails on this one?'
- Give verbal examples, 'it's like when you …'. Think these out ahead. They don't pop into your mind by magic.

Summarise

- Draw together what has been learned as you go along, e.g. 'So far we have found out these things', 'We know now the five main ways of …'.
- Summarise main points at the end.

Check for understanding

- Look to see if the children seem to be attentive.
- Ask questions to check that the children are following the explanation.

Finally, know your material. You will enjoy explaining things that you feel confident about. If you aren't sure, read about it, ask about it, learn about it.

If you are explaining things to pupils whom you anticipate will find a task especially difficult, the same rules apply. There are certain things that you need to be especially careful about.

- Break the task down into very, very small learning steps, interspersed with practice time and opportunities for reinforcement.
- Introduce the activity with plenty of reference to the children's own experience, e.g. 'This is like when at home you hear the kettle click off and you know – well, now, you tell me about what the water will be doing'.
- Take your time; don't appear rushed, even if you are! If you need to move on, explain what you are doing and say when you will be returning to give another input., e.g. 'I'm off to work with Janet's group now but I will be back by the time you reach number 4, to see how you're getting on. I think you'll be able to manage these for now'.
- Accept some responsibility yourself: 'I don't think I explained this very clearly. Let me try to do it again.', *or* 'I'm going to give you something hard, but I know you'll try your best and I will help'.
- Include lots of repetition, saying the same thing in different ways.
- Model steps within the activity for the children to imitate and join in with you. For example, 'So, we put two in this set, see? I've put two in here. How many have I put down? That's right, I've put two in. So how many do we have now? Now, let's see, how many more will I need? Yes, I think we need another four. How many? Yes,

another four. That's it, isn't it? Now for the next one…'. Gradually fade out your input as the children appear confident.
- Use gesture, touch, physical cueing and prompting to nudge and jog their memory and offer lots of intermediate steps along the way. For example, 'It's the curly letter isn't it? The one we learned yesterday, you remember, the one we said had to go all the way to the top and back again'.
- If you are presenting the task in workcard or worksheet form, talk about key ideas and specialist words *before* you read the sheet together.

Instructions

Many explanations are combined with instructions to make up an introduction or conclusion to a session or a focused teaching session with a small group or individual. The elements of an effective set of instructions are very similar to those of an explanation.
　Instructions should be:

- carefully sequenced
- in small steps
- simply stated
- appropriately spaced over time

To achieve this you may have to defer giving certain instructions and feed them into the session at a later time. As we have seen, order and sequence are important elements of both explanation and instruction and when these are combined in an introduction getting the order right is not easy. (Activity 2 in Section 2, pp. 106–8 gives you some practice at this.)

Questioning

Asking useful, productive questions is a skill that you must work at developing during your training. There have been plenty of indications in this chapter so far of the significance of questioning as a teaching tool both in its own right and as a contributor to other teaching techniques. It allows you to pitch explanations at the right level, to check if you are holding the children's interest and to monitor their learning. By using questions you can check for understanding at the end of a set of instructions or a phase within a demonstration or discussion, and use pupil responses to questions to build up a picture for the children of what they have learned in the consolidation phase of a lesson or activity. Skilful questioning also has a crucial part to play in the assessment process as you will see from Chapter 5 and helps you to make judgements about how effective a piece of teaching has been – although you must be careful about making assertions about the learning of individual children from a question-and-answer session with the whole class.

To become good at questioning you need to practice a lot; you also need a sensitive ear, a readiness to look at and (literally) listen to yourself as you teach, and a determination to listen to what the children have to say even if you are anxious, nervous or surprised at their responses. You also need a basic understanding of how questions are framed and utilised by teachers in the classroom context.

Questions are part of the very idiosyncratic 'language of classrooms' that you learned as a pupil and will find you adopt almost intuitively as a teacher. You should try not to lose sight of its uniqueness, though. For instance, when was the last time you asked a question of somebody to which you already had the answer? When did you last tell a friend 'Yes, good. That's just what I was looking for'? The rules of classroom talk and the nature and function of teacher questions has been the subject of considerable classroom research. (See Brown and Wragg, 1993.)

You will discover that teachers agree that they ask questions for the variety of different purposes as outlined above: to find out what has been understood or remembered, to reinforce learning, to manage or control situations and children, and to encourage children to think about what they know. This last category has been found to be used less often by teachers than any other function of questioning. As well as being classified by *function*, teacher questions are also classified by *type*. 'Open/closed' is one useful dimension, 'open' referring to those questions to which there can be a whole range of responses, 'closed' referring to those to which there can be only a single response, often of one word. Another dimension is that of 'recall/thought'. Factual questions are those that ask for recall of fact or information whilst 'thought' questions look for a measured response that expresses an opinion, an idea or personal point of view. Most importantly, 'thought' questions enable the learner to create new knowledge and understanding.

It is tempting to see all 'open' or 'thought' questions as 'good' questions, and recall questions as always of the 'closed' variety. A minute's thought will recognise that this is not so: for instance, a question that asks 'How many different types of animal did we see at the zoo?' is an open question in that there are a number of legitimate answers. Yet it is also a recall question that does not *require* the children to think about the meaning of their response, nor to make connections with prior or future learning. 'What is special about this creature's ears that tells you he might hunt at night?' is a question that requires both observation and thought to answer – a 'thought' question in fact. However, there is only one fully acceptable answer which makes it a 'closed' as well as a thought question.

Sometimes student-teachers feel anxious about using the full range of questioning, as in this example from a student-teacher's classroom. She had pinned up an enlarged street map of the local area and her intentions were for the children to:

- notice and remember how various features, e.g. buildings, roads, the local canal, etc. are represented on a local map
- understand the need for consistency of representation
- be able to locate and use a map key

The session began well enough, with the children identifying the map as one of their local area. However, it did not progress as the student-teacher, Melanie, had hoped. Wishing very much to build upon the children's own ideas and allow them to tell her what they knew, she asked open questions such as: 'What do you notice about this map?', 'What can you tell me about this map?' which allowed the children to tell her that it was a map, that it was a big map, that it was a map of Southport – but not that it depicted buildings, roads, etc. in a particular way. The children did not know which aspects of the map they were to attend to. Fortunately, Melanie was monitoring the level of response and quickly realised her lack of progress and began then to ask more sharply focused questions such as:

- 'What are these dark-coloured rectangles showing?'
- 'Can you find Lord Street?'
- 'What do you see crossing the road here?'
- 'What do you think the lines might mean?'

Now the children were able to observe and make a direct reply to this much more 'closed' questioning which required both observation (of the map) and recall (of other maps they had seen, of what previous experience tells them of what is likely to be marked on a map).

Practising questioning

Practising questioning is the only way to become better at it. It is not easy at all; in fact it is a very challenging aspect of your training, quite a risk-taking business for you. To get the wording right you must plan out your questions very carefully, so that you know in advance the questions you wish to ask and have decided upon a sensible order in which to ask them. However, children will not respond predictably! This means that unless you ignore their answers, you will not be likely to be able to stick precisely to your carefully planned-for sequence of questions – very unnerving. Also, you need to give the children sufficient time to think of their answer. Again, this can be quite alarming to the new teacher in school as it requires you to be the listener and to tolerate silences. Above all, to be an effective questioner you need to be able to listen, really listen, to what the children have to say – not easy when you are feeling a little unsure, have firm intentions for learning in mind and know what it is you want to hear.

Let us consider, then, how you might increase the number of open/thought questions that you ask and begin to properly listen to what the children have to say. A good way to begin is to focus first of all upon questions that you will ask in order to elicit the children's *own ideas* (not the answers which you anticipate). To be effective these will be worded so that they:

- let the children tell you what they know
- usually have an answer that isn't simply 'yes' or 'no'

- first give the children the opportunity to observe carefully
- encourage the children to think about and use knowledge they have acquired
- encourage them to solve problems and plan tasks for themselves

When questioning in this way you should:

- look and sound interested
- give the children enough time to think of their answer
- ask the questions in a sensible order
- and *listen to what the children say*

All of this means that you must plan your questioning carefully. When you are planning out your questions, *think to yourself*:

- What do you want to know?
- Which questions will help you find that out?
- Which order will you ask the questions in?

The example in Figure 4.4 shows how you should first decide what it is you want to know about the children's ideas and understandings. Then you can devise questions worded so that you can find this out.

You will notice certain things about the questions in Figure 4.4.

- These questions are child-centred, that is, they are worded to find out what the child knows/understands/has noticed about a situation rather than to find out whether the child knows a particular answer.
- They are helping you build up a clear picture of the children's understanding, and that will help you teach them effectively – you need to know what they need to learn.
- When you listen to a child's answers, you may find you want to ask some additional questions to find out a bit more.

The next thing for you to develop is the ability to question in order to encourage children to solve problems and plan tasks for themselves. Again, you need to plan out the exact questions you intend to use, thinking to yourself:

- What do you want the children to notice, think about, see as interesting to explore further, investigate?
- What questions will focus the children's attention and ideas in this way?
- What will be the best order to ask these questions in?

Ways of asking questions

The way in which you conduct a questioning session is just as important as framing your questions properly to suit your learning intentions. It is very easy to believe that a question/answer session has been successful because a handful of children have eagerly contributed. You need to think about how many children participated in some

Imagine you wish to use a poster of a Victorian kitchen with a group of 7-year-old children,	
What do I want to know?	*Which questions shall I ask to find out?*
● What room do they think the picture is of?	Where do you think this is a picture of?
● What have they noticed to help them decide?	What is it about the picture that made you think that?
● Are they aware of the period portrayed?	Have you any ideas about when a kitchen would look like this?
● What have they noticed to help them decide?	What gave you some ideas about that?
● How do they think the role of women then compares with that of today?	Who would you expect to find working in a kitchen today?
etc.	

Figure 4.4 Planning for questioning
Note: We are indebted to Dorothy Watt of the University of Central England for this example.

way, how you encouraged this by your body language such as smiling, nodding, encouraging, signalling interest, drawing children in by saying their name, putting a finger to your lips to stop over-eager interruptions.

Try to monitor the effectiveness of your questioning technique when it is used as part of an introduction, or parallels explanation or instruction. The checklist in Figure 4.5 will help you to do this.

Modelling

Modelling is a very under-valued teaching skill, perhaps because it is less readily described and is rather similar to demonstrating. In fact, it is a different skill, in that the teacher-message is not: 'Watch and listen carefully and I will show you how to do it'. It is rather an unspoken message of: 'Notice how I am doing this. It seems to be a good way of working, doesn't it? Shall you try it, too?'

In a modelling situation the teacher uses methods, techniques, skills, modes of speaking, displays attitudes, that are so successful or appealing that the children will adopt them for themselves. Some examples from earlier in this chapter will help you to see this.

For instance, in Joanne's Mathematics lesson, she traced along the horizontal, then the vertical axis with her finger each time, without comment, but so that the children were able to note how this helped her to locate the correct point on the grid.

In Steve and Diane's lesson, their teaching input with the tape-recording group would be principally one of modelling. Rather than giving instructions, they would sit with the group and contribute to the discussion, taking care that their comments

Checklist questions	Comments
Did I try to involve all of the group?	
Did I make sure all were attending?	
Did I make good eye-contact and alter the tone of my voice appropriately?	
Was the vocabulary appropriate to the group?	
Could all the children hear?	
Did I give enough time for the children to answer?	
Were my questions asked in a logical order?	
Did I listen to answers and use these in subsequent questions?	
Did the children ask each other questions?	
Did the questions challenge the children and make them think?	

Figure 4.5 Questioning checklist

reflected the attitudes and skills they wanted the children to develop. In order to help the children identify and then use for themselves the features of a good description (specificity being one feature) they might say: 'I can really tell very well who that person was because it tells me about the very thing that we all like about Tariq so much, the way he always smiles when … That detail helped me a lot.'; *or* 'Now, I think in my message back to Penny I want to tell her first of all what I liked about her description of David so much.'

In this way the children are learning from the teacher to look for and identify specific cues, that detail is valuable in a description *and* that in giving feedback to their peers they should try to start with the positive features.

Modelling is a very powerful teaching tool. Teachers use it intuitively all the time, but you can *learn* to apply it systematically, too.

Giving feedback

Giving feedback to pupils during lessons is fundamental to teaching well in primary classrooms and you should actively plan to use this teaching strategy. You may think that giving feedback can only happen spontaneously, but like all other teaching skills, its full potential is realised if you are pro-active about it and plan carefully for its use.

Feedback is a genuine response to the learner specifying *why* something is well-done or has been understood or satisfactorily completed. Feedback helps to reinforce learning as it takes place, during the lesson and also through marking or responding to outcomes in other ways. To give effective feedback, you have to plan to manage and organise your time in order to be with different individuals and groups at different

Learning Experience	Teacher's role	Resources	Assessment indicators
Look at examples of clockwork toys. Think about what makes them move. Does anyone know? Why do they slow down?	Ask questions. *Encourage* speculative comment and shared responses. *Praise* speculative comment.	Four different small toys with key mechanism.	Do the children see that winding up the toy is important? Do they notice as it slows down? Do they 'think aloud' about it?
Demonstrate how to make a crawlie tank, showing how to wind and fix the elastic band.	Demonstrate clearly, showing the stages on diagram on chalkboard as I explain the steps. *Reinforce* accurate recall of stages: praise.	Large-size cotton reel plus diagram on board ready.	Can the children recall the stages? Can they say which bits will be difficult? Do they ask their own questions? Can they start without fussing?
Children working in pairs to complete the tank. Threading elastic band through cotton reel. Twisting tightly around the matchstick. Keeping the matchsticks steady and balanced.	Move between groups *helping* and trying to sustain construction by *praising* efforts. Point out/model tightly wound examples. Help with manipulative aspects.	Cotton reels, elastic bands, matchsticks enough for one between two.	Do the children manage to feed the elastic band through the holes? Do they twist the band tightly? Do they help each other by holding things steady, etc.?
Try out tanks. Compare movement. Notice influence of length of matchstick.	Suggest trials. Ask questions about differences/similarities. Say *how well they have done.* Help children finding it difficult.	Strips of wood as 'runways'.	Do the children start the tanks at same point? Do they observe how they move? Do they notice if the stick impedes movement?
Discussion about what makes the tank move.	Ask why the tank moves? What have they noticed? What makes a good mover? Listen out for key words to *reinforce.* Where is the energy stored? How do they know?	Collection of completed tanks.	Do the children say that the wound up band is tight/taut/full of energy? Do they explain clearly why they think it moves? Do they use the term 'energy'?

Plan 4.3 Example of a plan to encourage feedback to the children

times during the lesson, as did Steve and Diane in their small group approach. You also have to be reactive, like Martin wished he'd been, and address the whole class to offer feedback and constructive criticism. Sometimes this can be spontaneous, at other times it happens when and as you plan for it to happen, as in Dawn's lesson shown in plan form (see Plan 4.3).

In this lesson, Dawn is using cotton reels and elastic bands to help the children construct a 'tank' that moves forward when the energy from a wound up elastic band is released.

As you can see, Dawn planned the lesson to include a great deal of regular and systematic feedback. Her intentions were that the children would understand the concept of stored energy by making a 'crawlie tank' from a cotton reel, matchstick and elastic band, which she anticipated many children would find difficult. Because of this she decided to give ample feedback at each stage of the lesson, as shown in the 'teacher's role' column.

She is, you will note, very precise about the nature of the feedback – this is not a vague praising of effort but a positive reinforcement of the skills and understandings that she wants to develop. For instance, she notes that she will praise speculative comments in the introductory phase of the lesson, which is the main intention for learning at this stage. You see that later she identifies the principle of fair testing as the feature that she will reinforce through comment, questioning and praise.

You may think that this makes the task of planning even more demanding! In practice, you will find that as you work out your assessment cues you will be reminded to plan for when and how you will give feedback. Think to yourself:

- As I see/observe/hear the children in this situation, how will I give them feedback so that they know whether they are making progress?
- How do I intend to give feedback on the outcomes or products of the session?

In the plan above, Dawn was prompted by her assessment indicator of 'do they twist the elastic band tightly' to note that she would point out tightly-wound examples to the other children. In the concluding stages she was looking for the use of particular terms to indicate to her that the children understood how the crawlie tank moved. She notes in the teacher column that she will reinforce these key words – by repeating them, using them again later, writing them up on the chalkboard and so on.

In implementing this plan, Dawn found that the children needed even more help with the manipulative aspects than she had thought, and a number of pairs seemed to despair! Dawn gave the children lots of praise and practical assistance, encouraging them to persevere by telling them that she was sure they could manage the task, even though it *was* very tricky. She found that by praising children who had managed to thread the elastic band, they were spurred on to the next step and the other children tried even harder, in the knowledge that it was actually possible. Spontaneous and planned-for feedback greatly helped in the implementation of this activity.

Enhancing the learning experience

We have already seen in Chapter 2 the powerful messages that the classroom context can convey. The ways in which you invite or direct children to become involved in tasks and the appearance of the classroom itself are as significant to the children's learning as being an effective questioner or explainer. So we need to think about:

- classroom display
- resource areas/centres of interest
- workcards and worksheets

all of which support your chosen Teaching Approaches.

Classroom display

The primary classroom should say, 'Welcome – we enjoy it here: good things are happening.' It should reflect the on-going work, interests and enthusiasms of the class, so that a visitor entering would know at once the subjects and themes under study.

You will find, too, that because children learn from everything that is around them, they will be more involved, interested and participate more fully if the classroom environment is stimulating and attractive.

Do – make your displays interactive. Display is integral to teaching and learning so build in:
- time for the children to work with a display;
- space around the display to allow for groups of children to work there;
- questions and activities to direct attention and suggest active response.

Do – display mainly children's work, encouraging them to make certain decisions about how it should be arranged.

Do – allow display to grow. Work in display need not be complete; you can display first drafts, working notes, etc. Aim to get work up quickly and make sure that you have the nature of the task made clear by a suitable heading.

Do – be disciplined about the use of colour. Don't introduce too many colours and coordinate them to give the display unity.

Do – make headings for the display that have lots of impact and keep all your lettering neat and even. If you are not confident about your lettering, use a word-processor and enlarge on a photocopier.

Do – cut all edges with a commercial trimmer. Nothing looks worse than wobbly edges. Be exact about spacing, too: lay out the items for a display in front of the board and move them around until you are satisfied with the arrangement. Use a measure to check width of columns and blocks of displayed items. Fix samples on with Blu-Tak until you can fasten permanently.

Do – use a staple gun rather than drawing pins or Blu-Tak. If you have to use the latter, be prepared to do running repairs and don't fasten up anything too heavy or too large.

Don't – try to rush. Display is time-consuming, but you will be well rewarded by the children's enthusiastic response.

Don't – leave display up until it becomes faded and torn.

Don't – forget headings.

Don't – forget to include the children's names.

Don't – be put off if you find display difficult at first. You will learn quickly with lots of practice.

Figure 4.6 What to do with displays

There are many useful books about classroom display. All we have room for here are a few simple 'do's' and 'don'ts' in Figure 4.6.

Resource areas

You have already thought about the impact of space upon the learning environment in Chapter 2. As you saw, young children learn best if they are in a secure, affirming ethos, in a physical environment where each individual is valued and their learning time is maximised. One way to achieve this is to rearrange the classroom to accommodate small groups working in particular 'areas' or 'corners' using specialist equipment and resources. Even if your classroom is small you can set up such areas with books, paper, pencils apparatus and the like, as discussed in Chapter 2.

Workcards and worksheets

Well-designed worksheets are really important teaching devices that help you to achieve your learning objectives. You need to treat them with caution, as in themselves they often are not sufficient to promote learning. Consider both sides of the argument below.

Worksheets can:
- help you to match the task to the capabilities of individuals and groups of children
- relate the task precisely to the materials to be explored
- provide essential practice and opportunity to record the answer without unnecessary writing
- provide a structure for recording responses
- help children to access information otherwise not available to them
- act as a classroom organiser by giving instructions and questions to initiate activity whilst your time is elsewhere

Worksheets can't/shouldn't
- replace direct teacher intervention and focused teaching
- answer the question for the children
- of themselves ensure a high level of presentation; you will have to moitor this carefully
- necessarily foster independence of thought
- teach information retrieval skills
- act as your replacement; they are an extra source of learning support

If you decide to make a workcard or worksheet, you must then think carefully about its content and design. There are some general rules to bear in mind.

- sketch the layout in pencil, using an underlying grid to help keep lettering straight if you need it

- lay out the sheet so that different sections are slightly spaced out
- try to include pictures or other visual clues to catch attention and make it look interesting
- avoid an overcrowded worksheet
- leave a clearly identified space for a name
- indicate clearly where the responses are to go
- always use the handwriting style of the school

You will of course need to use a range of strategies for presenting activities to children who find learning more difficult. They can still be helped through workcards and worksheets so long as you match the reading level comfortably to their level of achievement. Here are some further points to bear in mind when designing printed material for children who are not fluent readers.

- make sheets clear and uncluttered
- use black on white
- keep sentences short – one line long
- use small case letters
- enlarge the print
- keep the print going from left to right – no columns or clever layouts
- have nice wide margins
- keep the sheet short: not too much information at once.

CONCLUSION

This chapter began by showing that effective teaching in the primary school involved you, the teacher, in making daily choices about 'fitness for purpose'. As you plan your teaching you should consistently ask yourself certain key questions that will help you to choose well, questions that reflect the three strands of primary teaching, the child, the curriculum and the school.

- Will all of the children be able to manage this learning experience? Will it be sufficiently demanding for them all? Will some children require extra attention and support?
- Which aspects of the activity will need focused teacher intervention, i.e. explanation, demonstration, questioning – and will this be the same for everyone?
- Which aspects of the work will I need to ask thought-provoking questions about, or extend the children's ideas on?
- Can I foresee points in the lesson when some or all of the children will want to ask questions?
- Will I be able to look for evidence of learning?

SECTION 1: BACKGROUND

Primary Needs Programme 1985

Primary Needs Programme (PNP) was launched in Leeds to meet the needs of all children, especially those with special educational needs living in disadvantaged urban environments. A sum of £14 million was provided to

- increase staffing ratios
- provide INSET and extra advisory support
- increase capitation
- refurbish shabby buildings

Recently published documents on primary education

'Report of the Evaluation Team, 1991', Prof. Robin Alexander, of Leeds University. Its findings were as follows:

- reading standards did not rise
- unbroken cycle of 'low expectations and unchallenging curriculum experiences' for socially disadvantaged children
- curriculum unduly weighted towards the Core
- unintentional focus on teachers' classroom practices, especially 'multiple-curriculum-focus-teaching'
- teachers felt under pressure to adopt classroom practices which they did not always believe in

'Curriculum Organisation and Classroom Practice in Primary Schools: a discussion paper'. (DES: Jan. 1992), Robin Alexander, Professor of Primary Education, Leeds, Jim Rose, Chief Inspector, HMI, Chris Woodhead, Chief Executive, NCC.

Outcome of an eight-month 'enquiry' into the state of the nation's primary schools. Argued for:

- selection of organisational strategies, i.e. class, group or individual, to meet criterion of 'fitness for purpose'
- deployment of range of teaching techniques, e.g. questioning, explaining, instructing, assessing, diagnosing, giving feedback
- thorough planning as essential to successful teaching
- the place of both subject teaching and clearly-defined topic work
- the need for specialist teachers, especially in Key Stage 2
- the importance of regular assessment of pupil progress
- a higher level of task demand

OFSTED report (Office for Standards in Education) 'Curriculum Organisation and Classroom Practice in Primary Schools: a Follow-up Report' (Jan. 1993a). Based upon discussion of issues and HMI survey of 74 primary schools (Jan. 1993).

'Commentary' noted:

- teacher concern about 'curriculum overload'
- shift towards topics more focused on a single subject
- insufficient exploitation of the benefits of class teaching
- the 'small but significant' growth in semi-specialist teaching

In Appendix B the following are cited as associated with 'better classroom practice' in the survey schools.

Organisational strategies

- Carefully planned and appropriate grouping of pupils for tasks
- A mixture of individual, group and class teaching
- A manageable number of teaching groups and learning activities, usually four or fewer, provided in the classroom at any one time
- Carefully planned use of the teacher's time for giving instructions, teaching the whole class, individuals or groups, and
- moving between activities to instruct, question, explain, assess (i.e. focused teaching)
- Clearly established classroom routines and procedures

Teaching techniques

- The use of good oral instructions to set the scene and explain tasks to the whole class or to a group
- Opportunities provided for pupils to raise questions about tasks or activities and for the teacher to listen to the pupils
- Skilful questioning to encourage children to think and use knowledge already acquired
- The observation of pupils at work to help with assessment; careful and regular monitoring of pupil progress
- Teacher interaction and purposeful intervention in pupils' work
- Appropriate use of teacher demonstration
- The use of good work by pupils as a model for others
- Teaching targeted to specific individuals or groups
- Appropriate praise and encouragement
- Feedback to pupils during lessons
- Continuous assessment as an aid to the learning process
- Criteria for assessing work made explicit to children

'The National Curriculum at Key Stages 1 and 2: (1993)' – advice to the Secretary of State NCC.

A hard-hitting report that states that overload is leading to 'superficial teaching', lacking in rigour and challenge.

Recommendations include:

- more subject teaching
- more focused approaches to topic work

and, in relation to organisational strategies,

- different approaches to classroom management, including a suggestion that class teaching is currently undervalued
- the setting of pupils according to ability, when practicable

---

SECTION 2: ACTIVITIES

Activity 1: Small-group work/focused teaching

A class of twenty-nine Year 6 children have newly set up a 'fitness centre' in the activity-area of their open-plan classroom as part of a unit of work on 'Health Education'. It contains an exercise bicycle (loaned!), a small exercise-circuit for press-ups, 'stepping', sit-ups, etc. Stop-watches, tape-measures, height and weight charts have been collected, together with information books and a variety of leaflets on diet, smoking, alcohol and drug abuse. So far, one group of six children has trialed the exercise circuit.

See Figure 4.7, the organisational plan for the morning.

Action

1 Plan out in detail, using the more detailed lesson plan format, how you would introduce this session to the whole class and then to each group.

Think carefully about how you intend that each group will:

- know why they are doing the activity and what they are meant to learn or practice
- relate their task to the work of the whole class
- know where to collect their resources (a plan might help here)
- understand the requirements of the task, i.e. 'what to do'

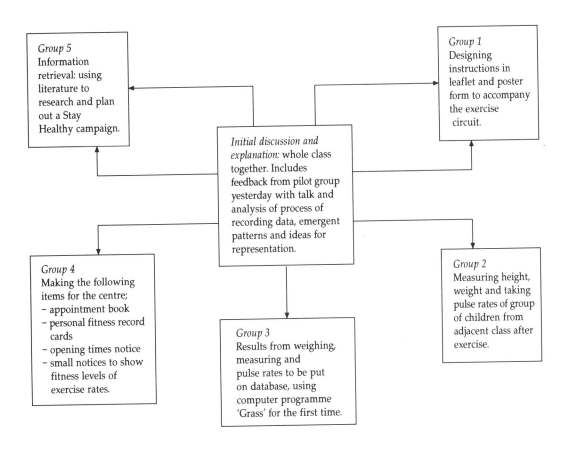

Figure 4.7 A plan for small-group work

- know how long it should take them
- be aware of when you intend to join them
- know when they have 'finished' and what will become of the outcome

2 Decide which group(s) will be *L* (low level of teacher input); *M* (medium level of input); and *H* (high level of input) as the groups start work following the introduction. Will this change as the activities progress? If so, how?

3 Decide upon the teaching strategy for your focused teaching time with the L, M and H groups, thinking about and writing down in detail how your explanations, instructions, questions and feedback will vary according to the differentiated needs of the groups.

4 Make an instruction-type workcard for the L group(s) to help them get started and to continue on task.

5 Devise a way of letting the children know what they should do if or when they have 'finished'.

Activity 2: Sequencing an explanation

The following Figure 4.8 is an example of an out-of-sequence introduction.

Setting

The children have watched a video-clip of the period 400 BC–300 BC, showing the Persian Wars, including the battles of Marathon and Salamis; the supremacy of Athens under Pericles; the Peloponnesian Wars between Athens and Sparta. They are now to construct a time-line from 500 BC to 350 BC showing the main events in picture, date and written-label format.

Objectives

1 The children will be able to recall the names, dates and outcomes of the main battles, as seen on the video.
2 They will use reference /information books to supplement their knowledge.
3 Working in groups of four, they will accurately construct a 20-year segment of the line, marking on key events.

If possible, carry out this task with a fellow-student, as a pair

1 Decide

- upon the order in which you would present the separate parts of the introduction shown above.
- upon the teaching strategies that you would use at each stage: demonstrating, explaining, questioning, instructing. Tick the appropriate box.
- the visual aids or teacher-made resources that you would require.

2 Compare with your partner

- Can you agree a sensible sequence?
- Have you got a balance of teaching strategies, e.g. questioning, explaining, instructing, to involve the children as much as possible?
- Would you add anything to this 'introduction'?

Activity 3: Practising questioning

(We are indebted to Dorothy Watt, University of Central England for this activity.)

This activity should enable you to talk with children, to find out their ideas about an interesting object, and will allow you to practise your questioning techniques.

You will need to arrange to work with a small group of three to four children for some fifteen minutes and take to school with you:

What the children will need to do, know, understand, find out about, decide, discuss, etc. (These are the 'answers' to the teacher's 'planning questions'.)	Zero	Explan-ation	Instr-uction	Demon-stration	Order of Intro-duction
Know that resource books will be positioned at sides of classroom.					
Decide which aspects of task are allotted to individual group members.					
Write the years in felt-tip, over pencilled draft.					
Be able to measure out line into equal segments.					
Recall events of Persian Wars as on video.					
Remember that important dates are on blue card on white, illustrations on white on gold, written information white on yellow.					
Scribe the dates in correct chronological order for BC.					
Search and select from reference books to supplement recalled data.					
Know that they are to construct a time-line to show key events.					
Know what a time-line is: that a certain distance equals a set number of years.					
Know that the completed time-line will be consulted regularly as work on Greeks continues.					
Remember that written information for a 'display audience' needs to be drafted and revised before publishing.					
Know which section of the time-line their group is responsible for.					
Be aware that the activity should be completed by the end of the afternoon.					

Figure 4.8 An out-of-sequence 'introduction' to rearrange

- an interesting object
- your list of questions which you will have prepared earlier
- a cassette recorder
- a blank tape.

Ask your classteacher if you can talk to a group of children in a quiet area, as you will be tape-recording the discussion. Before you start, show the children the tape-recorder, maybe demonstrating it to them. Tell them you will be using it to tape-record what you and they are talking about. (Make sure you remember to start the cassette recorder!) Begin by allowing the children a short while to familiarise themselves with the object. When they appear to be at ease, use your list of questions to structure the discussion. Remember that it is the children's ideas that you are after, rather than a set of right answers, so be sure to listen to what the children are saying to you. By listening, you may decide to add some extra questions as well, but try not to let the discussion go off at too great a tangent. Draw the discussion to a close when you and the children have said what you want to say. When you get back to college, listen to your tape critically.

Decide:

- which of your questions worked well at encouraging the children to give you ideas. What features do they have in common?
- which of your questions were least effective. How could you have worded these questions more effectively?
- how well you listened to the children. Did you pick up on interesting ideas they presented? Were there any questions you would like to have included? How would you word these differently to be more effective?

ANNOTATED BIBLIOGRAPHY

Alexander, R. (1991) *Primary Education in Leeds: Twelfth and Final Report from the Independent Evaluation Project, Leeds*, Leeds University.

Alexander, R. (1992) *Policy and Practice in Primary Education*, Routledge.
Based upon the reports of the Primary Needs Programme, this is a rich and intensely thought-provoking book. Read Chapter 4 'Teaching Strategies' especially for questions and queries about:
- *teachers' use of pseudo-questions*
- *teachers' reluctance to direct, inform, explain*
- *the nature and quality of pupil–teacher interaction*
- *what constitutes 'good practice'*

Brown, G. and Wragg, E.C. (1993) *Questioning*, Routledge.
Based upon information collected through the Leverhulme Project, this workbook:
- *looks at the different types of questions teachers ask (Unit 2)*
- *uses transcripts to illuminate the text*
- *in Unit 4 shows you how questioning can contribute to particular Teaching Approaches.*

Dean, J. (1992) *Organising Learning in the Primary Classroom*, Routledge.
Chapter 6 gives an overview of different teaching strategies and includes an interesting section on 'discussion'.

DES (1992) *Curriculum Organisation and Classroom Practice in Primary Schools.*
This has been summarised on pp. 102–3. It is a seminal text and will repay careful reading. For 'teaching' look especially at pages 27–34.

Kyriacou, C. (1992) *Essential Teaching Skills*, Blackwell Education.
Read Chapter 3 'Lesson Presentation' in particular. This chapter:
- *reviews explaining things and questioning*
- *class and individual working*

Moyles, J. (1992) *Organising for Learning in the Primary Classroom*, Open University Press.
Read Chapter 4 in particular. Dealing with grouping children for learning, it:
- *offers practical suggestions for getting children started on activities*
- *examines group composition in relation to intentions for learning*
- *considers the advantages/disadvantages of ability/mixed/friendship groups.*

National Curriculum Council (1993) *Planning The National Curriculum at Key Stages 1 and 2*, NCC.

OFSTED (1993a) *Curriculum Organisation and Classroom Practice in Primary Schools: a Follow-up Report*, OFSTED.
Published as a summary of responses to the discussion paper, this booklet:
- *explores further key issues (see summary above)*
- *contains in Appendix B 'Factors associated with better classroom practice' some telling points about effective primary school teaching.*

OFSTED (1993b) *Well-managed Classes in Primary Schools*, OFSTED.
What it says! Well worth obtaining and reading. The summary gives a full list of features of well-managed classes.

Wragg, E.C. (1993) *Explaining*, Routledge.
An entire workbook devoted to helping new teachers 'master the art of explaining'. There are activities to try out in support of each Unit.

5 ASSESSMENT, RECORD KEEPING AND REPORTING

In this chapter you will:

- explore the differing strategies open to you as a teacher to assist you in assessing children's learning, identify and practise specific assessment techniques and examine their relevance and appropriateness for particular activities

- examine the cyclic nature of planning and assessment and the importance of your identified 'intentions for learning' within the assessment process

- examine various ways of recording your assessment of children's learning

- learn about the various purposes of assessment and the different types of assessment used to meet differing purposes

- learn about the legal requirements associated with assessment and reporting

IDENTIFYING EVIDENCE OF CHILDREN'S LEARNING

In Chapter 3 on planning you examined carefully the planning process and realised that if your planning was to be effective you had to start from *what* you wanted the children to *learn*. This stage in the planning process is of tremendous importance in the subsequent assessment of the children's learning because if you have no *intentions* for your pupil's learning at the start of a session you will have no idea, except perhaps a general impression upon which to base inferences, *what* the children have learnt.

So, of course, the big question is *how* do we as teachers know that the children have learnt what we intended them to learn, and/or if they have, in fact, learnt other things besides? It is important here to remember that in planning you will have identified: the content of the learning; the knowledge you wish the children to acquire; the processes by which they will acquire that knowledge; the values and attitudes the learning process will promote.

Each activity that any teacher/trainee teacher plans contains different teaching/ learning experiences. They choose to provide particular experiences for certain children at certain times because of the learning opportunities such experiences can offer. In other words, we plan with the intention that childen will learn certain things from certain activities – these are our identified learning objectives. In the light of this let us re-examine the lesson planned, as an example for you, as the first session in a series of sessions on 'soil' on p. 42. In identifying the intentions for learning it was decided that the learning objectives would be:

- on the basis of observation and previous experience classify soils according to different criteria
- use previous knowledge to make hypotheses

How, then, was it planned to assess whether those specific objectives had been achieved? Was it intended to assess whether *all* the children had achieved those objectives or just a specific group of children?

In order to examine how the identified assessment indicators could provide evidence of the learning that had taken place and assist the teacher in identifying the possible outcomes, let us investigate what each assessment indicator actually means. Each assessment indicator is a prompt as to what to look for during the teacher's observations of the children at work and/or in the completed writing/drawing. Both of these are the possible outcomes of the children's learning.

The first part of the activity plans for the children to 'observe some examples of soil and share these observations with the class'. In the planned discussion that is intended to enable the children to share their observations, you need to note:

- who volunteers information in order to assess who, if anybody, has some previous knowledge, such as the fact that soil is made up of small particles
- whether the children's responses alter after they have heard other children make a contribution, such as 'oh yes and some particles are smaller than others'
- whether the children's responses alter after they have heard you make a contribution, such as 'What happens if we wet this soil?'

You will then need to make note of those children who are basing their responses upon observations of the soil samples they have been looking at. Your interpretations of your observations serve as the assessment of whether or not the children have achieved the planned objectives. In this case there is no *recorded* outcome by the children themselves but their verbal contributions to the discussion are indicators of their learning and therefore outcomes of the teaching/learning session.

After the children have collected the soil from different parts of the grounds outside, it is planned for the children to use magnifiers to examine the soil and make comparisons. Here you would not only be noting the responses to your carefully planned open questions but you would be examining the 'short precise notes' the children were making as these would be the written outcomes of their observations and further evidence of the learning which had taken place. During this part of the lesson it is imperative that you are cognisant of your learning intentions so that you can make judgements about whether the children have established 'different criteria' to classify the soils and who within the groups has been leading the learning. This part of the lesson develops into each individual child drawing, from observation, the soil samples they have collected. This, in turn, will provide concrete evidence of whether each child has understood the differences and is able to reproduce those differences in this way. Some childen may find it more dificult to draw than to verbalise their observations and vice versa. This will provide the necessary evidence about whether the children have observed carefully what they have seen and whether they are able to draw any conclusions from their observations and so begin the classification process. It is imperative that you offer the children both outcomes, that of drawing and that of talking about what they have seen, so that you do not close the door to any evidence of learning that is available and thus make inaccurate judgements about individual children's learning.

In the concluding part of the teaching/learning session you would again listen to the children's responses to questions and analyse their contributions to the class discussion about the qualities of soil. Here you yourself would act as a scribe for the whole class recording what they say and thus have a further record of the children's learning in a different form.

Plan 5.1 is an example of a differently planned teaching/learning session for a class of twenty-eight Y2 children. This shows that whatever the age range and classroom organisation, assessment is still an integral part of the planning process. It also provides a further example of a teaching/learning session to enable you as trainee teachers to consider how the assessment is linked to the identified intentions for learning.

Let us now examine the assessment indicators identified in Plan 5.1 and discuss how you, as the teacher, can gather the appropriate evidence of learning and assess that the learning has taken place.

> What evidence will provide us with the knowledge that the children have begun *'to understand about the chronology of time'*?

This evidence will be found in the responses to your questioning of the children, such questions as 'How do we know that Kelly is older than Ahmed?' It is also necessary to be aware that you might get some unexpected responses here, like the fact that Kelly is taller than Ahmed. This might be the case, but height is not an age indicator and needs responding to in the appropriate manner. Listening to the children who report back about the information they have found out will also provide you with the evidence you need to show that the children have understood the concept that there is a chronological sequence to events which we call time. Such statements as 'when we looked at the registers of Y3 we found that Janine's birthday was the same day in June as Tazir's, but we know Tazir is older because he was born in 1986 and Janine was born in 1987, a year later'. Such responses in conjunction with observation of the children at work, and analysis of the final recorded written outcome, i.e. the time-line, will provide evidence of the learning which has taken place.

TEACHING/LEARNING SESSION: . . . .   DATE: . . . .

HISTORY

Identified Learning Intentions
- To begin to develop an understanding about the chronology of time by examining a sequence of events which are relevant to their everyday lives.
- To develop investigative skills/retrieval skills, so that children can begin to interpret evidence from primary sources, in this case the class registers.
- To work cooperatively in a group, in order to complete a given task, through contributing ideas and listening to other's ideas.

Learning experience	Teacher's role	Resources	Assessment indicators
Talk to the class on the carpet area about their ages.	Explain	Flip chart Felt-tip pen	
Establish who is the eldest and who is the youngest, record this on flip chart, leaving space for all children to place their respective birthdays.	Question		Response to appropriate questions to demonstrate understanding
Tell children when your birthday is. Record this, on the flip chart.			
Draw children's attention to the difference in years between the eldest and youngest child and the difference in decades between yourself and them.	Explain		
Divide children into groups of four and give each group a specific task.			
(i) to divide a long piece of paper into six equal areas and each area into ten equal spaces and then divide each tenth into twelve	Instruct and explain	Long piece of paper, felt-tip pens	Written and drawn outcomes
(ii) to establish ages of teachers in the school		Pencils, notebooks	Written outcomes
(iii) to find out who is the eldest and youngest child in school			
(iv) to record all the birthdays of the children in their class from register		Register, pencils, notebooks	Modes of children's interaction
When the groups have gathered their respective data and recorded it all on the time-line the class will discuss the outcomes after individual children have reported back to the whole class what they have found out from their investigations			Written outcomes, responses to questions, listening to children reporting back to the whole class

Plan 5.1 Example of a teaching/learning session with assessment indicators

What evidence from the planned learning/teaching session will show you that the children have begun '*to develop investigative skills and retrieval skills*'?

By observing the group of children retrieving data from the class register, and analysing the information recorded in the time-line, you will be able to gather the necessary evidence of whether the childen have achieved this learning objective. Children would be recording the names of pupils from their class and putting all the children born in the same month in a group and then sequencing them in order of the days of the month. Watching how the children attack this task, analysing how they have recorded it initially and then transferred it on to the time-line, the final written outcome provides further evidence of the learning taking place. It will also be important to analyse the children's verbal reports of their findings, to the whole class, noting whether they have placed all the children in the correct chronological order and listening carefully to their explanations of *what* they did and how they did it.

How would you gather evidence of the fact that the children were able '*to work cooperatively in a group*'?

This could only be gathered by careful observation by the teacher of pupil interaction with each other. You need to ascertain whether all the children contribute suggestions for completing the task. This can be judged if, for example:

- they ask questions, such as 'how do we know Naomi is older than Amy?' of each other and/or the teacher, readily and easily
- they listen attentively when other children are making a contribution to the group discussion
- they select the equipment and share the tasks democratically, or, whether one child emerges as a leader

This list is not exhaustive and contains some of the examples that you could focus upon.

The link identified above between your planned intentions for the children's learning and the assessment indicators you intend to use to see if that learning has taken place clearly highlights the integral nature of the planning/assessment cycle.

EXAMINING ASSESSMENT TECHNIQUES

As is evident from the two examples outlined in this chapter so far it is possible to gather evidence of learning primarily in three ways. You can focus upon:

- the actions the children take (what they do) – such things as how they arrived at their decisions about classification in the lesson example on soil
- their responses to your questions or their contributions to discussion (what they actually say) – such as the answers about Kelly and Ahmed in the previous example
- the actual product of their learning in terms of writing, drawing, models, paintings,

etc. (what they actually record) – such as the time-line and the 'short precise' notes in the examples outlined above.

Any one of these sources of evidence can be examined in isolation, all together, or as a combination of any two of the three. This, however, does not paint a totally realistic picture because any analysis on paper is devoid of the obvious complexity of classroom life outlined in Chapter 2. What you need to be reassured about is that there is no definitive formula for successful assessment, but a range of opportunities and possibilities which vary from context to context. You have to give the best you can to assessing whatever is available to you within particular contexts. You must not, however, lose sight of the fact that you have a certain amount of control over those contexts when planning the learning/teaching sessions. This control over the context allows for your control over the assessment techniques you choose to use.

Some activities do not have any written outcomes, whereas others are primarily concerned with recording things on paper. However, such a focus does not exclude a dialogue taking place between the child and the teacher about the recorded work, but it is you who needs to make the judgements about whether initiating such a dialogue is appropriate at that point in time in your busy classroom.

There are other methods, besides teacher/pupil dialogue, of listening to what children have to say; you can listen to children talking to one another in groups, to one child talking to another, and to children reporting back to the class as identified in the example given (see Plan 5.1) for a teaching/learning session for a Y2 class earlier.

Planning activities which are full of potential for enhancing children's learning right across a range of processes, skills, knowledge and understanding is part of the armoury of every effective teacher today. If the demands of the tasks you plan are such that they provide rich and varied learning outcomes they will inevitably, in turn, provide you with appropriate foci for assessment. This being the case, there is no need, on most occasions, to plan specifically to carry out assessment. For as the SEAC (Schools Examination and Assessment Council) School Assessment Folder states, 'assessment is the *continuing* process of judging individual children's work' (our emphasis). Assessment is clearly a part of the day-to-day teaching/learning processes which take place in your classroom and all you need to do is make it a systematic part of that process when planning for children's learning.

THE MANAGEMENT OF ASSESSMENT

Whom to assess

Lets us re-examine the teaching/learning session planned for a Y2 class earlier in this chapter (Plan 5.1). How could you, as the teacher, hope to contribute to the necessary teaching that that session entails as well as the assessment of all twenty-eight children.

In most situations it is totally unrealistic to expect to assess all the children in your class at any one time. Who you choose to assess at any particular moment is inseparable from how you manage and organise your classroom and how and whether you group children. Different aspects of classroom management were discussed in Chapter 2 and you need to think carefully about how you wish to assess and what assessment techniques you wish to deploy when you select the particular teaching style and classroom organisation for a particular teaching/learning session.

If you want to assess through observation of children working by listening to them talking to one another then a 'whole class' approach would be inappropriate. However, if you have decided that in this particular case your assessment will be based solely upon an outcome recorded on paper, a 'whole class' approach might be appropriate. Remember you can always vary your approach according to circumstances but, realistically, and in most situations, it is best to focus on no more than four children at a time.

How to manage assessment

If we then focus on four children taking part in the outlined teaching/learning session on history, which four should we choose and why would we choose them? In the example referred to, it would be quite legitimate to focus your attention upon the group of children retrieving information from the registers and assess whether they have achieved your identified learning objective associated with the development of retrieval/investigative skills.

Follow a pattern of planning to assess a group of four children each day over a period of two weeks, i.e. ten working days. This will enable you to assess an average class of thirty-five children. It also provides you with some flexibility in order to cope with the inevitable unexpected event in a primary classroom.

The very nature of a primary classroom and the organisation of the curriculum, will mean, if you follow this plan, that you will not necessarily be assessing all the children on the same activities but on what you have planned for the teaching/learning activity for that day. This is not a major concern as effective assessment is firstly concerned with the formative process, the process of building up a profile which supports individual learning over a period of time. It is assessment which will inform your future planning for those children's future teaching/learning experiences.

This, again, emphasises the fact that assessment of children's learning and progress is central to effective teaching and learning and should be an integral part of that process. As we have stated previously, and cannot state too often, the purpose of the assessment must be determined by the original purpose of the learning experience planned by the teacher. Decisions about how to assess will be easier if the purpose of the teaching and learning and assessment are clear. Assessment needs to be an integral part of the teaching/learning process because the progress learners make is dependent upon a thorough understanding of the learning which has taken place, so that further learning can be planned for based upon strong foundations. So whatever the teacher plans for the learners in his/her charge must be founded in the previous knowledge and understanding that those particular children have. This has implications for the teacher in terms of their analysis of their part in the teaching/learning process. Did s/he manage an appropriate match? Was the planned activity an appropriate vehicle to achieve the intentions for learning or would some other method have been more appropriate? These are questions that need asking especially when learning objectives have not been achieved, so that the necessary action can be taken when planning further learning.

Planning for assessment

Sometimes, however, it may be necessary to plan an activity which is purely for the purpose of assessing a particular group of children in a particular area. This needs to be done so that the teacher can monitor progress across the class and ensure that the areas of learning which have not been assessed, but need to be, are assessed so that further learning can take place. Ways of planning such an activity could include the following.

1 Choose an activity.
2 Highlight the range of learning opportunities provided by the activity.
3 Decide which specific skills to assess.
4 Identify the National Curriculum element to be assessed.
5 What type of evidence do you need to support your assessment?
6 How will you gather this evidence?
7 How will you record the assessment?
8 What will you do with the information?

All the above are sound criteria for planning any teaching/learning session but have particular relevance when you are planning to assess a specific area of learning.

Let us now apply steps 1–6 outlined above to another teaching/learning session specifically designed to assess the children's learning in a Y1 class who are studying buildings. As part of the topic on buildings the children have visited a building site and looked at the building that was taking place. In order to assess whether the children have understood what processes are necessary to make the wall strong and safe you are now going to design an activity (see Plan 5.2).

We have spent a great deal of time, quite rightly, exploring the processes of assessment but now we are going to focus upon the other two topics of this chapter: record-keeping and reporting.

1	Choose the activity	Let the children, in pairs, build a wall with interlocking plastic bricks.
2	Highlight the range of opportunities provided by the activity	Discussing, cooperating, sequencing, exploring
3	Decide which specific skill to assess	Sequencing
4	Identify the National Curriculum element	Maths Key Stage 1
5	What type of evidence do you need to support your assessment?	Observation, finished product
6	How will you gather this evidence	Participant observation and notes about how the children approach the task
7	How will you record the assessment	Initially in a diary form, then on an appropriate record sheet
8	What will you do with the information	Keep it to form part of the child's summative record at transition and use it to inform future learning

Plan 5.2 Example of an assessment activity

RECORDING AND INTERPRETING EVIDENCE

How you record the assessment will inevitably be influenced by how you have gathered the evidence and what you will ultimately do with the information. Let us then examine some of the most common reasons why we assess.

- to plan – pupils' future performance after recognition of their positive achievements
- to diagnose – pupils' strengths and weaknesses so that we can match the learning experiences to individual children's needs
- to grade – in order to assign pupils into groups
- to evaluate - the effectiveness of teaching methods in order to structure, analyse and refine the learning experiences we offer
- to inform – parents, colleagues, other professionals about children's achievements

Record-keeping is the written outcome of the assessment process. It is vital to effective teaching and learning, as part of the 'planning/teaching/learning/assessing' cycle referred to previously and now shown in Figure 5.1.

Records that track the achievements of individual children will inform class-teachers, tutors and headteachers of progress but, most importantly, they will help you to provide more effectively as you plan and teach.

In order to fulfil the purposes identified above, it is necessary to devise differing formats for recording pupil achievement and teacher assessment. An example of how you may record your teacher assessments is given in Figure 5.2. This method of recording is designed to enable you to record what you observe, hear, and see and is, we believe, a form which is adaptable for most types of assessments of individual pupils.

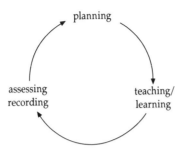

Figure 5.1 Planning/teaching/learning/assessing cycle

NAME: . . . . YEAR GROUP: . . . . DATE:		
Assessment indicators (Possible outcomes)	**Description**	**Judgements**
What you will be looking for. The planned outcomes of the teaching/learning session.	What actually took place. What did the child do, say, write, record or make?	What information does this give me about the child? What does that child know and understand?
Teacher action		
What does this tell me about my selected teaching strategies? How does this help my planning?		

Figure 5.2 An example of a teacher assessment form

Let us examine in detail what each of these sections on this particular recording sheet in Figure 5.2 actually mean in some depth.

Assessment indicators (possible outcomes)

Identifying the assessment indicators as part of your original planning process forces you to look back at the activities you have planned to identify the possible outcomes. If those outcomes do not give you the evidence you will need to judge whether the children have achieved your identified learning intentions, then you need to rethink your planned learning experience. The assessment indicators should be directly associated with your identified learning objectives, in other words, the one is dependent upon the other and is further proof of the necessity for good planning.

Providing a description

Giving an accurate description of what actually happened can be difficult and it is useful to keep a diary for notes of your observations when you first start to assess children's learning. As you practice observing children working, and recording your observations in this way you will become much more proficient at writing brief and pertinent notes. These, in turn, will enable you to make relevant and significant assessments and still keep the process manageable within the normal day-to-day 'hurly-burly' of classroom activity.

Making judgements

The description of the learning experience which you have recorded provides the evidence upon which you can make judgements about the children's learning. When you analyse it you must ask yourself what it tells you about what the children know and understand, what they can do and the processes they use to do it.

Teacher action

This part of the assessment process, deciding what to do with the information you have gained and what use to make of your judgements, is the completion of the circle in the planning assessment cycle. It takes you back to the planning stage of that cycle. It also makes you analyse how you tried to assist the children in achieving your identified learning objectives and whether your selected teaching strategies contributed to the children's success or lack of achievement. So the proposed teacher action can be twofold: it can either be what action you propose to take in terms of planning future learning experiences, or it can be concerned with how you organise and manage that learning. One action does not preclude the other and both can be dependent upon the other.

Let us now apply this recording sheet to a child who is a member of group A in the example of a teaching/learning session about the Egyptians given in Chapter 3 (p. 49) (see Plan 3.3). In this session there are three identified learning objectives:

- pick from a set of books one which will provide information about an identified area
- be able to use the index and contents page to find the appropriate section
- using the identified text pick one sentence which answers given questions

NAME: Winston	YEAR GROUP: Y4	DATE: 10.6.93
Assessment indicators (Possible outcomes)	**Description**	**Judgements**
Selection of appropriate texts to find out about how pyramids were built.	Winston was a little hesitant initially about looking at the books, but after Mary found a book and showed him the pictures on the front he began to look for himself.	Winston lacks confidence in a situation which initially appears to depend upon reading. But with help, not necessarily from an adult, he gained confidence and completed the task.
Active in using the contents page in order to find the right pages.	Winston was very keen to find some more pictures of pyramids and started flicking through the pages but Mary showed him how to use the contents page and he selected another appropriate text and found the correct pages by using the contents page.	Once motivated and interested Winston learnt how to use the contents page and applied this skill to another text.
Pick an appropriate sentence to answer the question 'who built the pyramids?'	Winston read the text out loud to the rest of the group. He found some of the words difficult but used appropriate phonic, pictoral and semantic clues to read the text. He also sought assistance from Mary. Together they selected an appropriate sentence.	Winston was gaining in self-esteem. He was achieving in an area he found difficult. He was using all the available clues to help him decode and find meaning. Winston demonstrated his knowledge about who built the pyramids by his selection of the sentence.

Teacher Action

Winston has developed some research skills. He needs more learning opportunities to consolidate this learning. He also benefited greatly from his peer tutoring and I need to plan more opportunities for him to be able to do this.

My choice of task and the pairing of Winston with Mary was a good teaching strategy as it enabled Winston not only to complete the task but also to learn how to do it. The fact he transferred this learning to a text of his own choice is evidence of this learning.

Figure 5.3 An example of a completed teacher assessment form

This example of recording your assessments (Figure 5.3) is not the only one available to you as a teacher. The Science Record in Figure 5.4 allows teachers to make comments about individual pupils' achievements, but does not allow for the evidence upon which the comments should be based to be recorded. Neither does it focus the teachers' thinking in terms of future provision for that child.

Sometimes it is possible to use a checklist to record what children have covered within the National Curriculum. Figure 5.5 shows such a checklist developed from the example in the teaching of co-ordinates (pp. 78–81). The table may be used as a skill-track so that each step is ticked off as the child shows competence and understanding. Such a detailed approach may be useful in tracking any learning difficulties.

SCIENCE REPORTS: Physical processes		
NAME:	DATE OF BIRTH:	
Area of study	*Content*	*Comment*

Electricity	1 Constructing simple circuits
	   – batteries, wires, bulbs
	   – buzzers
	   – motors	

	2 Understand the need for a complete circuit	
	3 Understand the use of switches and implement to complete and break circuits	
	4 Experiment with varying currents in a circuit	
	5 Draw different types of circuit diagrams	
	6 Construct circuits from diagrams	
Light	1 Understand circuits from diagrams	
	2 Understand that light cannot pass through certain materials	
	3 Understand and experiment with reflection of light	
	4 Explain the relationship between light and vision	

Figure 5.4 Example of a science recording form: Key Stage 2

REPORTING

The assessment procedures for the National Curriculum, and the content of that asessment is outlined in the 1988 Education Reform Act. In this part of the chapter, we have focused upon the vital elements of the legislation rather than getting bogged down in the nitty gritty of the actual administrative detaiis which, to date, have varied from year to year, and in the light of the Dearing Report will alter yet again.

The assessment of the National Curriculum core subjects, English, mathematics and science, and the foundation subjects history, geography and technology, have to

CO-ORDINATES	NAME:	
1 Recognise and name a mapping grid		
2 Explain how a grid helps with location		
3 Use word 'axis' correctly		
4 Differentiate and name horizontal and vertical axes correctly		
5 Be able to label axes correctly		
6 Recognise the need to number the axes		
7 Recognise that 0 must be the first number		
8 Correctly place other numbers in sequence		
9 Understand how to locate a point on a grid, tracing horizontal axis first		
10 Be able to record correctly, using brackets and comma		
11 Be able to give a grid reference for certain features on a map with grid		
12 Recognise the lack of precision in using 2-figure grids		
13 Understand how each square can be further sub-divided		
14 Know how to label a three figure grid		
15 Locate a point using 3-figure reference		
16 Name a feature using 3-figure reference		

Figure 5.5 Example of a checklist for Co-ordinates

date required teachers to take responsibility for two kinds of assessment:

- *teacher assessment* (TA). This is assessment of each element of the National

Curriculum, based upon the learning experiences which the children have had throughout their school year and summarised at certain Key Stages.
- *standard assessment*. This is assessment taking place at a specified time, using standardised assessment tasks (SATs) which in turn are designed to assess the learning of specific aspects of the National Curriculum.

Although in practice, thus far, in the primary school it is the teachers of Y2 and Y6 who have had the major responsibility for assessment of the National Curriculum the requirements, at present, for teacher assessment make provision for assessments which have taken place throughout the relevant Key Stage to contribute to the summation at the end of each Key Stage.

It is a legal requirement that teachers now report upon the achievements of their pupils annually. This takes the form in a lot of schools of an annual report plus the results of any SATs administered to the relevant age group. Reports come in many shapes and sizes but cover all the subjects of the National Curriculum. The individual results of any SATs that have been administered are confidential to the pupils, the parents and their teachers but results for a class as a whole and a school as a whole are to be available to the parents. It is also intended to publicly report schools' results for pupils at 11, 14 and 16; the publication of results at 7 is not mandatory but strongly encouraged by the Secretary of State. Reporting on schools' performance (DFE 1992) is structured specifically to allow comparative tables of school performance in public examination results at 15 and 17 and the collation of comparative information gained from the SATs will easily lend itself to such league tables even at 7+.

Some schools prefer to send out Records of Achievement to which pupils themselves have contributed. These are attempts to give that third dimension to what is essentially a two-dimensional picture, a summative record, a summary, of the child's achievements during the year. It is something which takes place at the point of transition and is informed by the formative assessments that have been ongoing during that year. Most schools like to make this a positive statement of the child's achievements and have moved away from the traditional styles of 'could do better', etc. to a more informative statement of what that child has covered in the National Curriculum.

CONCLUSION

We have tried to stress the importance of the assessment process as part of a planning/assessment cycle. If you follow the steps outlined below you will not only easily see how assessment needs to be an integral part of your teaching/learning sessions but also find a relatively uncomplicated pattern for ensuring you make it so.

1 Identify clearly your intentions for learning so that you are clear what you want the children to learn and what you will be assessing.
2 Choose which activity to observe. Some activities are 'better' than others; they

allow a wide range of children's skills and knowledge to become evident. Such activities should engage children's interest and further their learning.

3   Record the activity, briefly noting the skills, knowledge and process to be assessed, e.g. designing and making, following instructions, etc.

4   How will you gather this evidence? You may want to be an uninvolved observer or you may prefer to note their response to open-ended questioning. On other occasions the quality of the end product might record the children's abilities. Record the assessment method/s you decide upon in the most appropriate way.

5   Note which particular evidence you intend to use to support your assessment, e.g. examples of children's work, photographs, teacher-written recordings of children's responses to questions, tape-recordings of children's dialogue, etc.

6   Record the date.

7   Do not try to observe too many children in one session (one group of three to four children).

8   In general, comments made during or just after the activity are more helpful than grades or ticks against checklists. You may want to comment on the children's cooperative skills and may find making a list of such skills useful beforehand in helping you select which specific skill to assess, or in evaluating particular unexpected outcomes.

9   Share your assessment with the children and encourage them to be self-critical. With younger children this might be through discussion or a simple response sheet, while older children could be involved in recording their own achievements and setting future targets.

10   Note down any individual needs for extension or reinforcement that you have observed.

11   PLAN FURTHER ACTION.

SECTION 1 BACKGROUND

Significant issues, events and recent influences

1988 Education Reform Act

- Made testing at 7+, 11+, 14+ and 16+ a statutory requirement.
- Made it a legal requirement upon schools to inform parents of the results of the Standardised Attainment Test (SATs) results of their children and also the publication of 'league tables' by Local Education Authorities.
- Set up the Schools Examination and Assessment Council SEAC.

The Task Group on Assessment and Testing (TGAT) DES 1988

- Worked from the premise that there would be a National Curriculum with specific attainment targets at Key Stages.
- Perceived the national assessment system would run alongside teachers' continuous assessment.
- Identified a new concept: 'standard assessment task'.
- Identified the need to train teachers to moderate these tasks and also the need to train primary teachers in assessment across the full curricular range.
- Expresses a view that it is 'not satisfied that a sufficiently clear and coherent view of the primary curriculum now exists'.
- Finds it difficult to marry its brief with its members' obvious philosophy and experience.

1991

First SATs administered to Y2 children and first pilot tests at 14+.

1992

Amalgamation of the National Curriculum Council (NCC) and SEAC into one body, the School Curriculum and Assessment Authority (SCAA).

1993

First SATs to be administered to children of 14+ caused widespread unrest amongst the profession and an eventual boycott by the profession. Resulted in an acknowledgement by the Secretary of State for Education that the process was administratively unwieldy and led to the setting up of an investigation into the breadth of the National Curriculum and the nature of the tests led by Sir Ron Dearing. However, the boycott continued and there were no published results for either Y2 or Y9 children.

1993 (August)

Sir Ron Dearing reports and recommends a narrower curriculum for primary schools and 'streamlined' testing. This creates a fear within the profession of a return to the old style 11+ and 7+ tests of the 1950s/60s.

1994

Pilot test (SATs) at Key Stage 2 took place.

1994 Dearing Final Report

Published and accepted by the Government. Revised curriculum was published for consultation May 1994. New curriculum in place January 1995. Tests for 7-year-olds to focus on basic literacy and numeracy and, for 11-year-olds, English, mathematics and science. This begs the question, will the emphasis of the curriculum be skewed to the subjects which will be tested?

Forms of assessment

Formative and summative assessment

Some of the anxiety and suspicion that seems to surround assessment, springs from our confusion about the range of purposes it serves, and about the differences between 'formative' and 'summative' procedures.

'*Formative*': this term describes the process by which a child's progress and achievement is *assessed* and *recorded* continually as s/he moves through the school. It is the process which the majority of this chapter has been dedicated to and is what we believe to be a very necessary part of effective teaching. The TGAT Report (DES 1988, para 23) states that formative assessment is the process by which 'the positive achievements of a pupil may be recognised and discussed and the appropriate next steps be planned'. It is, in other words, the crux of the planning assessment cycle.

'*Summative*': this term refers to the summary of a child's achievements at a particular given time. This summary is based upon the 'formative' assessment that has

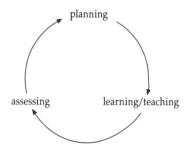

been part of the ongoing teaching and learning up until the point of summary. Often, however, summarising does not provide a full picture of an individual; it tends to place emphasis upon certain tasks at certain times.

In order to fully understand the quintessential distinction between summative and formative assessment it is necessary to examine the standardised national assessment testing required by the 1988 Education Act at 7+, 11+, 14+ and 16+. The 'Task Group on Assessment and Testing' (TGAT) (DES 1988) states that 'no system has yet been constructed that meets all the criteria of progression, moderation, formative and criterion-referenced assessment ... our task has therefore been to devise such a system afresh' (DES 1988, para 13).

The real issue is, in fact, whether it is possible to produce standardised tests/tasks which are both formative and summative at the same time. The TGAT Report itself lays its main emphasis upon summative assessment and although it tries to create a balance in importance between the two, it acknowledges that the report had to 'reflect the priority given in our brief to the need "to show what a pupil has learned and mastered"' (DES 1988, para 24).

It would seem then that the Standardised Attainment Tests (SATs) required by statute can only meet the summative assessment requirements and that although, idealistically, the formative assessment of children's achievements should be reflected in any summative reporting of their attainments, such 'scores' are not influenced by any of the formative assessment undertaken by teachers (Teacher Assessment). This being the case it is up to us as teachers to ensure that the formative assessment we undertake as an essential part of our daily planning for children's learning influences the other aspects of reporting children's achievements open to us, such as the now legally required annual report.

Types of assessment

There are three possible categories into which the judgements we make about children's learning may be placed: the norm-referenced assessment; the criterion-referenced assessment and the ipsative assessment. The differences lie in the distinction of what we decide to take as our yardstick.

Norm-referenced assessment

If we decide to compare a child with other children in the same year group or even with that wonderful creature, 'average child', we are making judgements against what is considered to be the 'norm', that is to say we are '*norm-referencing*'. This type of assessment has formed the basis of assessment in the British educational system and has thus inevitably formed the basis of our own experiences and that of the parents of the pupils we teach. As soon as 'norms' are established then we also establish a pass/fail bench-mark because a child's performance will lie below or above the norm. This type of assessment is designed to enable comparative judgements against other individuals; it is not designed to generate specific information about what an individual child knows, and is able to achieve regardless of what other children can do.

Criterion-referenced assessment

In order to glean specific information about an individual's learning strengths and his/her needs, it is essential to have a clear picture of what is to be learnt, i.e. your clearly identified learning intentions for that child or those children. The relevant assessment technique is then selected to provide the evidence, from each child, of whether those specific learning intentions have been achieved. In other words, the criteria for the child's success, is whether or not s/he has achieved what was intended. Criterion-referenced assessment measures the child's achievements against your predetermined expectations, i.e. your intentions for learning which were the starting points of your planning for teaching and learning.

Ipsative assessment

Another valid form of assessment is that process which measures a child's achievements from that child's own baseline, i.e. his or her starting point. It is most commonly used to assess an individual child's progress over a specified period of time. This type of assessment is more child-centred than any other form of assessment and provides an accurate picture of an individual child's achievements. For example, a child who enters school with poor oracy skills has made wonderful progress if by the end of the first year s/he is able to talk fluently about picture books. However, s/he may not score on any standardised reading tests.

Diagnostic-assessment

Another type of assessment you may hear referred to is diagnostic-assessment. This is often referred to in the context of establishing if something is 'wrong' in order to plan for appropriate remedial help. We would argue, however, that it can be any of the above forms of assessment as it is really the use we make of the assessment that has taken place that is the diagnosis for future action. It is the interpretation of the evidence we have gathered and the decisions that we make as professionals about the next step in the child's learning and our teaching. It is the link with the teaching that we lay emphasis on which removes the often negative connotations associated with diagnostic assessment because often what is seen as 'wrong with the child' is our failure to match appropriately the curriculum tasks we have planned. If we view diagnostic-assessment as that professional interpretation of the evidence and the educational experiences we plan in the light of those judgements, then we move away from the negative towards the positive and a much more enlightened approach to learning based in positive rather than negative reinforcement will take place.

Given that there are a variety of types of assessment and a number of differing purposes it needs to be stated that most formative assessment is aimed at assisting a child to progress. This is the case whether it is targeted at identifying positive achievements or by noting learning difficulties and is best achieved by teacher assessment and not by the use of standardised tests or attainment tasks. This is because such tests or tasks are in essence summative.

SECTION 2: ACTIVITIES

Activity 1: Purpose of assessment

With your mentor or fellow student colleagues identify the four most important purposes from the list below (which are not in rank order) and then list in order of importance your chosen four, 1–4.

1 to place pupils in rank order
2 to predict future performance
3 to diagnose specific weaknesses, with a view to specific provision
4 to provide a continuous record of achievement
5 to provide feedback on pupils' performance, and teachers' performance
6 to evaluate the curriculum being offered and the teaching methods employed
7 to increase motivation and self-esteem
8 to provide information about the pupil for colleagues and other interested parties
9 to inform the planning for the next stage of learning.

There is no correct answer to the above. It is an activity intended to illuminate the diverse opinion held within the profession and outside the profession about the primary purpose of assessment.

Activity 2: Common concerns about assessment

Take a blank sheet of paper and divide it lengthways into two columns. In the left-hand column write down some of the things that concern you about assessment. Now with a partner from your fellow teacher trainees or your mentor share two or three of your concerns for five minutes and then reverse roles. During your conversation note down in the right-hand column opposite the respective 'concern' about three or four points raised which you feel might assist you in the future. When you have finished share your thoughts with another couple, going through the same process. This will provide you with a support sheet for future reference.

Activity 3: Collecting evidence

Plan to watch a child closely at work, when you are observing your teacher/mentor teach.
    Now write down:

- what the intentions of the teacher were on this occasion
- what instructions were given to the pupils
- what were the precise activities of the pupils (e.g. measuring and recording the different reactions within a scientific experiment)
- what evidence became available as a result of the activities
    N.B. Evidence can be seen or heard.

From these descriptions now draw up a list which shows the activities and the evidence.

Activity 3: Listening to children

Tape-record a session you have planned with a group of children for a period of five minutes. Make sure this is a session where you have planned to question chidren. Now listen to the tape and analyse your interaction with the children and their responses. Is there any evidence of learning in their responses to your questions? Does your questioning aid or inhibit you in collecting the evidence?

Activity 4: Recording evidence

It is then essential that you as the teacher record the evidence you have selected. Use the suggested recording format in this chapter to record the evidence you have gleaned from the last activity. Then plan an activity with your mentor or tutor which is designed specifically to assess particular skills and knowledge and record your observations on the suggested format.

Activity 5: Making judgements

With the recorded description of the activity that you drew up in the last activity, now make some judgements about the children's learning from what you observed. What did the chidren learn? Did they achieve your identified learning objectives? If not, why not?

BIBLIOGRAPHY

Barrs, M., Ellis, S., Hester, H. and Thomas, A. (1990) *Patterns of Learning*, CLPE, London.

Dearing, Sir R. (1994) *The National Curriculum and its Assessment; the Final Report*, SCAA.

DES (1988) *National Curriculum: Task Group on Assessment: a Report*, Department of Education and Science.

DFE (1992) *Reporting Pupils' Achievements to Parents*, Circular 5/92, Department for Education.

Duncan, A. and Dunn, W. (1988) *What Primary Teachers Should Know About Assessment*, Hodder and Stoughton.

Gipps, C. (1990) *Assessment: A Teacher's Guide to Issues*, Hodder and Stoughton.

Manchester Education Committee (1990) 'Profiling for children of Primary School age', in *Manchester Schools, a Practical Manual; One Local Authority's Aid to Assessment. Recording and Reporting*, M.E.C.

Mitchell, C. and Koshy, V. (1993) *Effective Teacher Assessment*, Hodder and Stoughton.

O'Hear, P. and White, J. (1993) *Assessing the National Curriculum*, Paul Chapman Publishing.

SEAC (1990) *A Guide to Teacher Assessment, Packs A, B and C*.

SEAC (1992) *Assessment Folder 1993*.

Sutton, R. (1993) *A Framework for Assessment*, Nelson (2nd edn).

6 SELF-APPRAISAL THROUGH PROFILING

In this chapter you will:

- think about what self-appraisal involves and how it contributes to your professional development as a teacher;

- consider the teaching competencies against which self-appraisal can be set;

- try out ways of collecting evidence about your own teaching competencies;

- practice self-appraisal through profiling, target-setting and action planning.

WHAT IS SELF-APPRAISAL?

Self-appraisal is a positive action, a supportive and developmental process and it is *very* important that you think of it in these terms. It is not about pinpointing the *faults*, flaws and weaknesses of your teaching performance but rather about identifying your strengths and achievements as well as recognising areas for further development.

Self-appraisal is critical to the whole process of 'becoming a teacher' and to remaining an effective teacher throughout your professional career. Good teachers never stop feeling and acknowledging that there is more to be learned, as this very experienced teacher-mentor shows, in conversation with her student-teacher:

> Oh, I still feel like that! I still think, when we've had a really exciting session, will I ever get them back down? You always feel like that, even now. You have to remember all the different ways of doing it, and then you think afterwards about whether you chose the best way.

Like this teacher, the way you can best learn, build up and fine-tune your repertoire of teaching competencies is to look at yourself, appraise yourself regularly and quite systematically. You do need to remember, though, that at this stage in your professional development, the focus of the self-appraisal process will be upon the acquisition of those competencies vital for your success as a Newly Qualified Teacher. These will be the baseline competencies that you then build upon and extend in your first post and beyond. Training is no longer seen to finish after your initial qualification: rather, it is viewed as a continuum from initial training into the induction year through to life-long career development.

So the qualities of reflection and analysis will and indeed must be developed from the start of your training (see Section 2, Activity 1, pp. 157–8). They are fundamental to quality teaching and cannot be suddenly 'added in' at the later stages in your development, when you will certainly continue to need them. You will use them in the induction year, in order to benefit fully from the support network that you should find in your first school; you will apply them in preparing for the School Teacher Appraisal process that now forms part of the induction year; and you will use them as a life-long learner-of-teaching in order to set further professional goals. (See Section 1, pp. 155–7 for further details of induction, teacher appraisal and baseline competencies.)

As we saw in Chapter 3 on Planning, appraisal of yourself as teacher is a significant element of the planning feedback loop of:

You can see from Figure 6.1 how systematic and purposeful reflection and evaluation of yourself as teacher feeds directly into the planning loop to create a complete 'Teaching/Learning Cycle'.

The sequence of questions that makes up the inner 'reflection loop' in the diagram shows what self-appraisal involves. From Figure 6.1 you can see that in appraising yourself you will need to:

- in (1), identify and select *'critical incidents'* from your experiences in classrooms and training institution;
- in (2), *reflect* upon and analyse these critical incidents;
- in (3), determine what you have *learned* about yourself as teacher, about children as learners, about teachers and teaching;
- in (4), *apply* this learning by transferring it to other situations;
- in (5), *monitor* your progress systematically.

Here is a simple example to illustrate how the self-appraisal stages fit into and complement the overall planning cycle.

The 'teach' stage

Jenni, a student-teacher, groups the class together on a carpeted area to share a series of twelve slides of modern paintings, with the learning intention of comparing how different artists depicted form and movement. The children are most responsive, observant and questioning, and for the first thirty minutes, almost all the children are

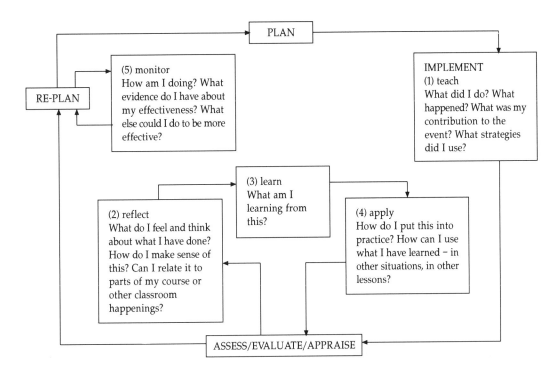

Figure 6.1 Teaching/learning cycle

totally involved. By picture number 8, their concentration lessens. Jenni persists with the lesson, and by the final picture, a group of children are quietly talking amongst themselves. Jenni has noticed this, and tries to re-involve them by asking them directly about the details on the final slides.

The 'reflect/self-appraisal' stage

At break-time, Jenni talks with her mentor and student-teacher partner about how she had noticed this drop in motivation. She says she 'wishes there had not been so many slides', but didn't reconsider showing them all. 'I felt it was in my lesson-plan, so I had to carry on'.

The 'learn' stage

Jenni learned that it is better to leave the children feeling positive and interested, even though some of her teaching points might not have been covered. She said that she should have responded to her own feeling that she had carried on for long enough, but had felt afraid to depart from her lesson-plan.

The 'apply' stage

Jenni decides that in her next lesson plan she will highlight the examples within her introduction that she could leave out if she feels the children have understood. In planning generally she aims to be much more selective in her choice and use of resource material, focusing her teaching points on fewer, high-quality initial stimuli.

The 'monitor' stage

Jenni and her mentor agree to scrutinise her plans for the next session for evidence that she has identified steps in the lesson that could be adapted or remain unused for the next session with the class. Jenni's mentor will observe this lesson, focusing especially on the introduction phase, in order to give specific feedback on first, her flexibility, and second, her ability to retain the attention of the children throughout the introduction.

Self-analysis plays a very important part in this self-appraisal cycle. It is *Jenni* herself who identifies the 'problem': she realises that this was a 'critical incident'. Her readiness to appraise her own performance and to discuss this after the lesson enables her to learn from it immediately. Jenni's mentor also has a significant part to play in the learning, advising and helping her to follow through the reflection and analysis into the learn–apply–monitor stages. Yet all the actions are Jenni's: Jenni decides, Jenni re-plans, Jenni asks for feedback. And when this feedback on the next lesson occurs, the whole cycle can begin again, with Jenni sharing her reflections with her mentor once more.

SELF-APPRAISAL THROUGH PROFILING

So far we have discussed why self-appraisal is important and have shown you something of what the process will involve. As you reflect upon and analyse experience you will wish to:

- share your ideas with your mentor on a regular basis
- organise your reflections in a systematic way
- record them within a framework of 'dimensions of competence'
- create an action plan or individual development plan

To help you in this, you will need to compile and regularly complete a *'Profile of Professional Development'*. This will be a document in which you make entries to record your developing competence as a teacher; it will give you a framework for reflection and enable you to structure and record your developing competence. We suggest you organise your 'profile' under five broad headings, which we term *'dimensions of competence'*. These were developed by the teaching team in the School of Teacher

---

Management for Learning

Note the significance of and begin to provide for:
- time: pace, flow, beginnings, endings, transitions
- people: roles, responsibilities, responses to pupil behaviour, equal opportunities
- resources: provision, accessibility, maintenance
- space: general layout, specific areas for learning

and then select from whole class, group and individual grouping to achieve:
- a balance of organisational patterns, matched to task and pupils' learning needs
- opportunities for children to practise and consolidate basic skills
- focused teaching targeted at individuals and groups
- groups of children engaged in exploratory/creative/investigative activities whilst the needs of the class are monitored and met
- high standards of behaviour, and positive attitudes to work, both in output and quality
- a range of strategies to deal effectively with different types of pupil behaviour

then extend the above to:
- include increasing numbers of children in self-supported learning
- foster purposeful collaborative group working

then create a classroom ethos that:
- can be adapted to different modes of teaching and learning
- enables children to make effective decisions and contributions to its smooth running
- allows equal opportunity issues to be addressed with confidence, openness and understanding

---

Figure 6.2 An example of a profile dimension

Education at Edge Hill College of Higher Education, and are:

- Understanding and Assessing Children's Learning
- Management for Learning
- Planning for Learning
- Teaching Skills
- Personal and Professional Development

Figure 6.2 illustrates what is meant by a 'dimension of competence', by showing aspects of professional development within the area of classroom management. (See Section 1, pp. 153–5 for details of all five dimensions.) How to use and set out the profile will be discussed later in the chapter. For now, notice the progression in terms of size of teaching group, and complexity of classroom organisation for which you will be responsible as you build up expertise.

Don't be put-off by the use of the term 'competencies'. This does *not* indicate what is sometimes referred to as a 'technicist' or 'reductionist' approach to learning-to-teach, with success related to a series of checklists of teacher behaviours. Rather, competence is to be seen as a dimension within the profiling system that we suggest, and as such, incorporates a number of significant features, listed as follows.

UNDERSTANDING AND ASSESSING CHILDREN'S LEARNING							
Note and begin to respond to: • the qualities and characteristics of young • learners • the ideas of children and the learning process of individuals	Date	Evidence	Date	Evidence	Date	Evidence

and then show competence in:
• recognising what and how children are
  learning, and adapt teaching methods
  appropriately
• indicating appropriate expectations to
  individual children
• selecting and using procedures for
  collecting assessment information
• making accurate assessment of the progress
  of individual children
• recording children's achievements (record
  keeping)						

then plan focused teaching for:
• the correctly identified and diagnosed
  needs of all children, including S.E.N. and
  gifted
• encouraging pupil self-assessment and
  target-setting						

then explore and practise:
• reporting of children's progress to parents,
  colleagues, outside agencies
• ways of advising school co-ordinators
  about own Subject Specialism						

Figure 6.3 Suggested layout for profile of professional development

- The recognition of *levels* of competence. You have seen that the statements within the dimension of 'Management for Learning' are hierarchical in terms of student-teacher achievement – they allow you to chart progression, which will be at a different rate for each individual student-teacher. You will also find that you move up and down the levels within each dimension because learning is not a linear process. Try to see the profile as an instrument that allows you to record the layers of experience and learning as you move through your course.
- The *complexity* of teaching. As we saw in Chapter 4, teaching *well* in the primary school is a complex business, involving:
  - an understanding of how children learn and develop;
  - a knowledge of the National Curriculum within the whole curriculum;
  - the ability to select appropriately from a range of teaching strategies to meet the requirement of 'fitness for purpose'. (OFSTED, 1993. See Section 1 of Chapter 4.)

- The *spiralling,* and *overlapping* nature of professional development. You will find that the dimensions overlap and on occasion an incident or piece of learning may seem to fit into more than one dimension. This does not matter – the important thing is that you record your progress somewhere in the profile. There are no 'right answers' in profiling.

The suggested profile format shown in Figure 6.3 shows how you might set out a profile. You can see that you have space to write down what makes you think you have made progress within a certain dimension, noting the date when this happened and your 'evidence' alongside this. You may also decide on future targets in this respect. This is a more sophisticated approach to profiling than a checklist 'tick box' approach, one which you may find difficult at first. Student-teachers who used a similar format wrote: 'I found it quite daunting at first – something you put into your file and tried to forget.' After a term of use, they were able to comment: 'It has helped me to think about what I have done in school and the processes I go through' *and* 'It has made me think, and know what I need to learn, and be able to evaluate myself.'

If you complete a profile regularly with your mentor, you will also begin to see and share together the goals towards which your training is aiming. 'The course ... has got a framework. The headings pull it together, give it structure. Those are the threads of the course, and I see it.'

USING THE PROFILE

Initially, you need to explore the dimensions of the profile in order to feel comfortable with them. This is best done in a supportive, group-learning situation, in which your tutor, mentor or classteacher and other fellow student-teachers participate. Within such a preliminary group situation, there will be certain features of 'profiling' that you will want to discuss and clarify before you start to make entries.

Students who have worked with a profile similar to the one we show say: 'Explaining the profile is really, really important. It makes all the difference if your tutor talks to you about it, and you discuss what the dimensions mean.'

A possible structure for such a session is shown in Section 2, Activity 2 (pp. 158–9), as are general ideas for 'getting started' on profiling.

Familiarity with the profile comes with use, however. As you work within it to record your successes, strengths and weaknesses, you will learn where to find statements that relate to a particular experience or newly acquired skill.

It is also a good idea to establish a set of *procedures* for profiling, ground rules that you, your mentor and tutor can adopt to make the process work to its best advantage. Some of the points and questions that you will need to clarify with your tutor and mentor are listed below. No doubt you will wish to add to this list to suit your particular context, because, remember, there is no single, 'correct' way to 'do profiling'.

- *Will you meet together with other student-teachers to discuss progress as a group as well as discuss your entries on a one-to-one basis?*
  Sharing your feelings and experiences with your colleagues can often make you appreciate more clearly what exactly it is that you have learned and feel confident and positive about yourself.

- *Will you use the profile to assess what has been learned during particular periods during your training, both college and classroom based?*
  Although the profile statements relate most evidently to classroom life, they will also relate to the 'taught' aspects of your course. Appraising what a group of student-teachers has learned within one or more profile dimensions can give structure to student/tutor group reflection and evaluation of a segment or unit of your course.

- *Will you create a timetable for profiling, for discussion and completing entries at set times/ points in your course?*
  The profile can help with debriefing following extended periods of time on school placement, for instance. There may well also be a place for timetabled college-based sessions devoted to 'profiling' on either a group or one-to-one basis. Alternatively, you may meet with other trainee teachers and their mentors in clusters of associated schools. Sessions devoted to profiling allow you to share your entries, help in setting targets and give the profile the significance it requires to be its most useful.

- *Will you make entries in the profile in an on-going fashion, as you reflect upon experience and have something to say?*
  It is usually more helpful to do this rather than wait until an appointed time for its 'official' completion.

- *Will your mentor share in this process? Will your college tutor have a role to play?*
  In a partnership situation, your mentor and your tutor would wish to share the profile with you, maybe making written comments in it in reply to what you have written.

- *Who will take the initiative in writing entries in the profile?*
  Will you always note the 'evidence' first, so that your mentor or tutor can 'reply'? Or will you sometimes invite another person to make an entry for you, following discussion or observation?

- *How will you set targets – by yourself, or collaboratively?*
  By discussing these issues you can determine how best to use the profile to suit your own situation. Above all, you should feel ownership of your profile; it is your means of making your progress in teaching explicit. By enabling you to record your own progress, the profile also encourages you to notice strengths, weaknesses and support needs. In this way, it gives you an effective learning tool to use throughout initial training and into your first post.

COLLECTING THE EVIDENCE

We have seen that the collection of appropriate 'evidence' is an important feature of self-appraisal through profiling – so the quality of this data must be high. We suggest four main approaches to data/evidence collection.

Self-appraisal schedules

Some events and incidents will be so formative that they will stay clearly in your mind for ever – and ever. For instance ...

> A certain beginner teacher many years ago inherited a hamster as a class pet. Each weekend the children left enough food and water to supply his dietary needs, which the teacher checked had been attended to at the end of Friday. One Friday, she forgot this check. On her arrival in the classroom on Monday morning, she was greeted by a muffled squeaking sound. She anxiously lifted the cover of his cage to discover the poor little creature shaking his furry head, encased helmet-like in an upturned conical yoghurt pot. It took the gentle expertise of the Deputy Head to cut the hamster free, and the monies of the school emergency fund to pay for a veterinary check-up. She has never forgotten this and is now obsessively careful about the needs of animals. In later years as a Deputy Headteacher herself, she also recalled the embarrassment of the 'note to all staff' circulated by the Headteacher later that particular morning, exhorting all teachers not to place animal food in inappropriately shaped containers. (Who could have been so foolish?)

You can decide for yourself what might make up a profile entry from this, if a profile had existed for this teacher then!

Many features of your development will not be so dramatic, we hope, and so you may need to use certain aids to reflection such as prompt-lists and cue-sheets. These act as personal reminders or post-event 'memory-joggers' of what occurred (helmeted animal); subsequent outcomes (personal distress, sick animal, accusing children, financial pain, professional embarrassment); and your reflection and consequent learning (always, always remember everything, and never, ever, send semi-public reprimands).

Prompt lists

We use this term for schedules that apply to your teaching in general and are not tied to a single profile dimension. They are useful in helping you to appraise yourself over a short period of time that has just passed. A useful general self-appraisal prompt-list as shown in Figure 6.4 involves thinking about what was said to you and what you had

---

1 What kind of things have you, the student-teacher, had to:
- ask about,
- note down,
- remember to do or say?

2 What responses have there been from the *children*?
- what have they said, to you, the teacher, each other?
- what have they done, work-wise and behaviour-wise?
- what have they made, written, drawn, modelled?

3 What kind of things has the *mentor/teacher* had to
- do, or not do?
- say or not say?
- explain?
- point out?
- remind you of?

Figure 6.4 Self-appraisal prompt-list

to ask about or felt the need to comment upon within a specified time span, of three to four weeks.

The evidence is collected from reflecting over a number of critical incidents and drawing out general conclusions. You could respond to a prompt-list like the one in Figure 6.4 and ask your mentor to do the same. You can then make a comparison of your results the basis of a profiling discussion.

School-based

- are you able to link your plans to what the teacher has in mind?
- do you want to know more about the children's capabilities as you set about planning your sessions?
- do you think ahead in order to ask the right questions about, for example, resources, groupings, space, timings?

College-based

- do you try to write down your intentions for learning before you produce detailed activity plans?
- do you 'have ideas' or do you usually have to search for these?
- do you get excited about your ideas for teaching?
- are you able to think things through on paper as if the lesson were happening in your mind, e.g. timing, questions, explanations?
- have you been able to use your 'assessment indicators' to gauge understanding? If not, can you decide why not?
- have you used or adapted ideas from curriculum courses?
- do you enjoy searching out ideas and information to help with planning?

Figure 6.5 Planning for learning: self-appraisal cue-sheet

Cue-sheets

These are self-appraisal schedules connected quite specifically with individual profile dimensions. They pose questions that should help you to make profile entries about both classroom and college-based work. Figure 6.5 shows one such cue-sheet for the early levels of Planning for Learning.

Figure 6.6 is a further example of a cue-sheet: for self-appraisal related to Understanding and Assessing Children's Learning. If you look at the statements within this dimension, shown in Section 1, p. 153, you will find that the questions relate to the second cluster of competencies within the dimension. The focus is on your developing expertise in assessing children's learning. The evidence you note will be your use of a variety of assessment strategies; and in deciding how often and in what way you *use* the assessment information that you collect, you are on the way to target-setting. Note, too, that you need to judge your personal understanding of public theories about assessment – an instance when entries in the profile reflect your grasp of key ideas and principles of teaching and learning. As you progress, you should always try to relate what you have learned in the classroom to theoretical perspectives. (See Section 2, Activity 3, pp. 159–60 for further ideas for using cue-sheets.)

School-based work

- how good are you at noting and taking advantage of assessment opportunities whenever they arise?
- do you regularly note down things about the children's achievements?
- have you attempted checklists to help with assessment?
- do you look at how the children go about their work, in order to judge its suitability and amend your future planning?
- do you use your observations and judgements to help you to plan?
- have you come to know what to expect of the children in your current placement class?
- are you able to reecognise those aspects of a task that particular children will find difficult?

College-based work

- do you understand the theoretical basis of assessment?
- do you use assessment terminology, e.g. 'formative', 'summative', etc.?
- do you know how to assess subject-specific process skills, e.g. observation, hypothesising in Science, use of primary evidence in History, designing in Design/Technology, etc.?
- are you suitably informed about National Curriculum assessment procedures?

Figure 6.6 Understanding and assessing children's learning: self-appraisal cue-sheet

Lesson evaluations

Your written evaluations of the lessons that you teach are another excellent source of evidence about how you are progressing and should trigger the self-appraisal process. A suggested format for lesson evaluation is shown above in Figure 6.7. This will help you to *analyse* the lesson rather than merely describe it. By reflecting first upon what

EVALUATION OF: . . . .   DATE: . . . .

Identified learning objectives
[The knowledge, skills, concepts and attitudes you wanted the children to learn.]

Analysis and reflection: children What did they actually do? What did the children learn? Were the learning objectives achieved? How do I know?	**Analysis and reflection: teacher** What did I learn? What did I do that helped or hindered the children's learning? How do I know?
• were the children interested and involved? • did the tasks match the children's capabilities? • did each child perform as expected? • did the children understand the key ideas? • did they know why they were doing what they were doing? • were they able to handle the equipment safely and purposefully? • were they pleased with what they achieved? **What 'evidence' do you have for your judgements?** Did you see the kind of learning behaviour you anticipated? Did you see the kind of outcome or product you anticipated? Did you have any difficulty in deciding what an individual child had achieved?	• did you keep attention throughout? • were your objectives sensible (e.g. too many, too few? too difficult, too easy? too structured, too vague?) • was the content presented in manageable learning steps, in the most appropriate sequence? • was your explanation clear? • did you use your voice effectively? • was timing satisfactory? • did the children have sufficient time to apply and practise new skills? • did you help the children to articulate and organise their ideas? • were you able to make use of and build upon the children's own contributions? • did you have sufficiently high expectations of all the pupils?

What are the *implications* for future planning, in terms of:
(a) progression in learning?
(b) for your teaching skills?

Figure 6.7 Example format for lesson evaluation

the children *actually* do and learn, you will consolidate what you have established from your assessment information. Then you can decide what you, the teacher, actually did that helped or hindered the children's efforts. Look for links between these two aspects of the lesson. This is made easier by the parallel children/teacher boxes. Don't feel it necessary to 'answer' every question every time you evaluate a session; rather, you should select those issues pertinent to the particular lesson or activity and to your learning intentions.

The implications section is especially useful in helping you to ensure that learning from evaluations of individual lessons is fed forward into future teaching – the teaching/learning cycle at work again. It is also a constant reminder to you to appraise your teaching skills, and referring this section to a series of lesson evaluations will help you in setting targets in your profile. It may be that you are also able to use your comments to identify a focus for classroom observation sessions, undertaken by either your mentor, tutor or student-teacher colleague. (See Activity 4 in Section 2, p. 160.)

Classroom observation

This is another most helpful way of obtaining evidence and feedback upon your classroom performance. There are two kinds of classroom observation situation discussed in this chapter. One is the '*spontaneous observation*' that occurs during any shared classroom teaching situation, or during discussion with teaching colleagues. Don't feel threatened by this. Although such observation will not have been officially negotiated, we all pick up cues about colleagues' strengths and weaknesses from working alongside them. You can use the situation to your advantage and respond to the feedback opportunities it offers. '*Structured observation*' is a more formalised observation situation in which the classteacher/mentor will 'sit in' on a teaching/learning session. You should also reverse the roles by asking your classteacher and/or mentor if you can observe them teach a variety of lessons. Time and again, trainee teachers say that they all too rarely have the opportunity to watch experienced teachers teach.

Spontaneous observation

Here a student-teacher like yourself may well be working with a group of children while the classteacher works with the rest of the class, a situation perhaps more likely to happen at the beginning of training. However, team work is an important aspect of primary teaching, so you should encounter various arrangements for working in team situations with teachers and student colleagues during your training. Observation of colleagues can occur quite naturally in this situation, and feedback can be informal, non-threatening and very productive because you can share in the two-way dialogue.

The profile dimension of Management for Learning is one that will be a ready focus for this type of less-formal observation and feedback; this is a highly visible aspect of teaching, one that teachers in training find themselves very concerned to 'get right' and one that is often used as a rough and ready guide to your overall competence by visitors to your classroom.

So how can the profile and the process of 'profiling' help you and your mentor to structure spontaneous observation and to record your development? Let us look at the first stage of the management dimension, when it is envisaged that you will be working under the close guidance of the classteacher, observing, helping and teaching small groups of children and, for limited lengths of time, the whole class. The teacher and mentor will be looking for clues as to your sensitivity to classroom routines and your ability to pick these up and work with them. They will also be looking for how you relate to the children and they to you, as a teacher rather than helper. The profile itself indicates that you should be able to:

Note the significance of and begin to provide for:
- time: pace, flow, beginnings, endings, transitions
- people: roles, responsibilities, responses to pupil behaviour, equal opportunities

- resources: provision, accessibility, maintenance
- space: general lay-out, specified areas for learning

Work on assessment criteria for student-teachers, undertaken with practising teachers, students and tutors at Edge Hill College of Higher Education, indicates the nature of the evidence within this dimension. This is what a group of classteachers would look for and discuss with their student-teachers in relation to Management for Learning.

Time – the student-teacher:
- picks up on and discusses teacher routines,
- makes time for routines, e.g. packing away, without having to be regularly reminded,
- checks that everything is satisfactorily tidied away at the end of a session.

People – the student-teacher:
- spots opportunities for getting involved, stepping in to activities without being directed,
- notices and comments upon children's behaviour and their attitudes towards tasks and activities,
- talks with individual children,
- sets up situations in which individual children can sustain a conversation with them,
- is approached by the children with confidence.

Resources – the student-teacher:
- asks about the location of resources,
- tries to think ahead about what they will need,
- does not leave collecting together teaching materials until the last minute,
- notices when the teacher spots and provides for a resource need,
- checks that apparatus has been replaced properly.

Space – the student-teacher:
- makes a plan of the classroom,
- locates activities sensibly, e.g. does not paint on the carpet area!

You will see from these teachers' list of criteria that how you interact with the *classteacher* as much as with the *children* makes a significant contribution to assessments of your professional competence.

Teaching Skills is another dimension in which the evidence for entries into the profile may be gained from spontaneous observation and discussion of what was noticed by either teacher, mentor or even fellow student-teacher. The profile indicates that you will work with small groups and on occasion the whole class in order to:

- gain attention and interest
- sustain involvement

- draw a session to a satisfying close
- explain, demonstrate, instruct
- converse, question, discuss
- praise, check, reinforce, support

In this dimension the evidence may be organised in the following way.

Attention and interest – the student-teacher will:
- ask 'how do I get the interest of these children?'
- talk about ways of settling the children down before starting the lesson,
- use a lively tone of voice and appropriate register,
- will bring interesting items into school to enthuse the children.

Sustaining involvement – the student-teacher will:
- notice when children have 'switched off' or are 'drifting away',
- raise with the teacher 'what to do if ...'

Drawing a session to a satisfying close – the student-teacher will:
- allow time for rounding off, checking for understanding, consolidating learning,
- make sure all the outcomes are satisfactorily completed and handed in.

Explaining, demonstrating, instructing – the student-teacher will:
- break down explanations into manageable steps,
- enable the children to begin the activity without further instruction or support from the teacher.

Conversing, questioning, discussing – the student-teacher will:
- find ways of getting to know the children,
- show that they value the children as people.

Praising, checking, reinforcing, supporting – the student teacher will:
- remember to give praise,
- recap on things the children have said,
- think about the children rather than themselves.

The group of teachers who worked on this dimension emphasised the important role that conversation with the student had to play. Talking with student-teachers in their classroom revealed to these classteachers whether the student-teacher was being *reflective*, asking themselves sensible questions and, most importantly, thinking things through in terms of teaching strategies. So through shared dialogue you will learn how your teacher sees you and at the same time gain valuable information upon which to reflect, appraise your own development and make entries into your profile.

Such spontaneous observation may not give a complete picture, of course. What is observed depends upon what catches the attention of the observer, in this case the classteacher. However, the aspects of teaching noticed may be transposed into a formal observation schedule as shown in Figure 6.8 in order to supplement or complement the picture.

Structured observation

This is a situation in which you and your mentor, classteacher or tutor negotiate the observation of a particular session or part of a session, using an observation schedule to structure the observation. The most productive use of this type of observation is when observer and observed agree *together* upon the purpose and focus of the observation, which is then limited to the specified aspects of teaching behaviour. In a supportive situation, systematic yet sympathetic classroom observation can be a rich and helpful experience, an aid to self-appraisal and continuing development.

To illustrate this, we can go back to the Teaching Skills dimension of the profile. Let us suppose that you are concerned about 'introductions', the explanation element in particular. You talk about this with your mentor and identify a teaching session in which you know you must give a clear, precise explanation both in terms of content and procedures. Together, you decide that a structured observation of the first ten minutes of the lesson would give you some very useful feedback in order to appraise your exact strengths and weaknesses. You can draw up an observation schedule that precisely matches your needs. Items from the spontaneous observation classifications might be useful in doing this – Figure 6.8 is a simple example. You can see that on this schedule there is space for a brief comment as well as a mark, say a tick, to indicate each time the category of behaviour was noted. An alternative would be an interval

Teaching skill/strategy	Noted	Comment
Uses appropriate tone of voice		
Settles the children in suitable space		
Uses stimulus material to gain interest		
Focuses attention on the task in hand at start		
Breaks down explanations into manageable steps		
Questions appropriately		
Recaps and builds upon what the children have said		
Gives positive reinforcement		
Varies the pace, flow and nature of activity		
Notices when children have 'switched off'		
Holds involvement in the task		

Figure 6.8 Observation schedule, teaching skills

schedule on which the observer makes a record at set time intervals of, say, thirty seconds.

A schedule like this must be used with caution, as it is open to all the dangers of such observation instruments, e.g. cutting out observation of non-scheduled behaviour, ignoring the context within which the events occur, distraction of the observed by the presence of an observer and so on. However, combine it with other forms of data collection and its weaknesses are counter-balanced by the sharp focus that it gives to the observation experience. (See Activity 3, Section 2, pp. 159–60.)

You will realise from this discussion that classroom observation is not a straightforward activity that necessarily yields accurate and non-controversial self-appraisal data. It can be very useful, none the less. We suggest that to get the best from this situation, so that feedback can be properly received and enrich the self-appraisal process, you need to get the ground rules right. The suggestions below should help with this.

- Make sure that both observed and observer understand the criteria by which observer judgements are being made. Working together on the profile in the light of response to prompt-lists, cue-sheets and spontaneous observation will help with this.
- The student-teacher's lesson-plan and intentions for learning should be given over to the observer in ample time for them to be read, assimilated and reflected upon before the observation session.
- As discussed above, the student-teacher should negotiate at least one aspect of the session on which feedback is sought.
- The mentor/observer should focus the observation *and the feedback* on particular features or stages of the lesson. The profile dimensions can help in the selection process. It is not helpful to attempt to note everything.
- The mentor should remain as unobtrusive as possible during the lesson. If they involve themselves with the children, observation will be less complete and the climate of the classroom as established by the trainee will be affected.
- At the feedback stage, the student-teacher should first of all be asked for their comments about the progress of the session before any further discussion ensues.
- Feedback should be immediately after the lesson, as full as possible and couched in positive terms.

Student-teacher/mentor talking together

An aspect of your development in which it may be difficult to appraise yourself without some help from others is your ability to relate to and interact with those with whom you work – your classteacher, mentor, student-teacher colleagues, other teachers within the school. We have seen that the way in which you open up discussion about professional matters is seen by classteachers as a very important type of evidence about your development, both in itself and for what it can indicate about your teaching

Do you/does the student-teacher:

- make regular and sympathetic observations of individual children and share these observations with the classteacher?
- ask the teacher direct questions about individual children?
- notice and comment when children behave in unexpected or interesting ways?
- recognise and ask about the differences between children in their response to experiences provided?
- appreciate that teachers need to know about individual pupil's learning patterns?
- try different approaches in recognition of individuals within the group, asking for classteacher feedback?
- seek out other evidence about the children, e.g. ask about pupil records?
- take the initiative in approaching the teacher or mentor?
- ask to compare the children's outcomes of learning with those produced for the classteacher?

Figure 6.9 A discussion schedule for student-teacher and mentor: understanding and assessing children's learning

competency. So you need to ask for feedback about how you interact professionally, to supplement other self-appraisal data.

Once again, the profile can assist you in this, by giving you a framework within which to work. You will note that the initial statements within Personal and Professional Development ask you to:

Identify strengths and weaknesses by:
- analysing teaching through discussion
- collaborating with teaching colleagues

The profile also helps in suggesting areas for discussion. One of the features of classrooms that makes an impact on student-teachers most forcibly at the start of their training is the wide range of individual differences in any one classroom, and classteachers find a lot to say to each other about individuals within the class. So let us see how the profile can help to guide this discussion.

Figure 6.9 shows a 'discussion schedule' for this dimension. At first sight it may look similar to the observation schedule shown previously, but it is different in three ways.

1 The incidents and actions it invites you to examine with your mentor are mainly about your interactions with them or the classteacher, rather than the children; it invites you and the teacher or mentor to reflect upon *the way in which* you notice, ask about and comment upon children's learning;
2 It is intended as a retrospective 'prompt list', an *aide-mémoire*, rather than a direct observation schedule;
3 It should be used to guide two-way discussion about your development as a communicator, rather than to direct feedback following classroom observation.

It is intended to give a structure for talk between yourself and your mentor and help you to evaluate your ability to interact professionally.

We have looked at four different ways of collecting data that will inform the self-appraisal process. We have shown how the profile dimensions can help in this process, both in structuring your thinking and in giving you a document in which to record your ideas and indicators of your professional growth. Try not to rely upon any one means of assessing your own development but, rather, use a range of methods as suggested in this chapter.

SELF-APPRAISAL INTO ACTION-PLANNING

Profiling as outlined thus far involves you in setting personal objectives or targets for action as the result of the reflective process. The next step is to decide how to go about achieving these personal learning objectives. If we return to the example of Jenni at the start of the chapter we see that this is exactly what she and her mentor did. They asked themselves:

Where are we now? Together, they selected a problem or an issue; reflected upon what happened; and most importantly, *made clear to themselves what had been learned.*

Where do we want to go next? The focus then was upon future actions. They decided how to apply Penny's learning, *by setting clear personal learning goals or targets.*

How are we going to get there? Together, they made *an action plan, to a realistic time-scale.*

How will we know if we've got there? By deciding upon sharply focused classroom observation, they *decided how progress could be measured.*

Jenni's action plan was short-term and not formally recorded. However, in determining forward pathways as the outcome of a profiling process, it is as well to set out a written Action Plan – sometimes referred to as a Personal or Individual Development plan. Figure 6.10 suggests one way of laying out an Action Plan which highlights all the essential features of such a plan. You could construct several layouts like this to keep with your profile in its wallet or folder, or on floppy disk.

A plan like this could be made at the end or beginning of a school term, a period

What	How	Who	When	How
am I aiming to achieve?	will I achieve my goals?	will support my learning?	will my progress be reviewed?	will my learning be assessed?

Figure 6.10 Example layout of an action plan

of school placement or a unit of the college-based work and involves decision making about a number of key issues:

- '*what* am I aiming to achieve?' leads you to ask next:
  'Which targets shall I select from the profile?'
  Certain targets will have more immediate priority.

- '*how* will I achieve my goals?' leads you to think:
  'What learning experiences will help me to achieve my personal objectives?'
  Think here about all aspects of your training course.

- '*who* will support my learning?' needs a decision about who will give the appropriate support:
  'Will it be my mentor? my student-teacher colleagues? the tutor of my college-based course?'
  The person you identify may differ according to your goals.

- '*when* will my progress be reviewed?'
  'Will I have a chance to see how I am doing?'
  Try to set exact dates and even exact times when a review can definitely happen.

- '*how* will my learning be assessed?' Will it be through:
  - classroom observation?
  - scrutiny of my planning file?
  - analysis of the children's work?
  - written assessment such as an essay?
  - or even a traditional examination?

By noting down the 'answers' to these questions, you lay out a forward pathway that has specific markers along the way to encourage and help you succeed in meeting your targets. You can then record these achievements on the profile document.

As you see, the whole process of self-appraisal through profiling and action-planning is an ongoing cycle. It should help you to become a life-long learner, who will *never* say to a teacher-in-training, '*Forget all that you learned at college. This is the real world now.*'

SECTION 1: BACKGROUND

Dimensions of competence

(as adopted by the School of Education, Edge Hill College of Higher Education, Ormskirk)

UNDERSTANDING AND ASSESSING CHILDREN'S LEARNING

Note and begin to respond to:
- the qualities and characteristics of young learners
- the ideas of children and the learning process of individual children

then show competence in
- recognising what and how children are learning and adapt teaching methods appropriately
- indicating appropriate expectations to individual children
- selecting and using procedures for collecting assessment information
- making accurate assessment of the progress of individual children
- recording children's achievements (record keeping)

then plan focused teaching for:
- the correctly identified and diagnosed needs of all children including S.E.N. and gifted
- the encouragement of pupil self-assessment and target-setting

then explore and practise
- ways of reporting children's progress to parents, colleagues, outside agencies
- ways of advising on children's learning within Subject Specialism and how it might be assessed, recorded and reported

MANAGEMENT OF LEARNING

Note the significance of and begin to provide for:
- time: pace, flow, beginnings, endings, transitions
- people: roles, responsibilities, responses to pupil behaviour, equal opportunities
- resources: provision, accessibility, maintenance
- space: general layout, specific areas for learning

then select from whole class, group and individual working to achieve:
- a balance of organisational patterns selected to match intentions for learning
- opportunities for children to practise and consolidate basic skills
- focused teaching targeted at individuals and groups
- management of groups of children engaged in exploratory/creative/investigative activities whilst the needs of the whole class are monitored and met
- high standards of behaviour, and positive attitudes to work, both in output and quality
- develop and extend strategies to deal effectively with different types of pupil behaviour

then extend the above to:
- include increasing numbers of children in self-supported learning
- foster purposeful collaborative group working

then create a classroom ethos that:
- can be adapted to different modes of teaching and learning
- enables children to make effective decisions and contribute to its smooth running
- ensures that equal opportunity issues are addressed with confidence, openness and understanding

PLANNING FOR LEARNING

Contribute to classteacher's daily planning by:
- producing simple but inventive complementary plans for the core National Curriculum subjects (class and group)
- clearly stating intentions for learning
- identifying assessment criteria

then produce medium-term and daily plans which:
- translate initial planning into learning objectives
- relate to the whole curriculum, National Curriculum Programmes of Study and Attainment Targets
- match content and teaching strategies to intended outcomes, age and abilities of the children
- show how assessment runs alongside teaching

then plan a coherent sequence of learning that:
- provides for breadth and balance and equal access across the range of primary curriculum
- responds to National Curriculum cross-curricular themes, dimensions and skills
- provides a differentiated curriculum for those with special educational needs

then consolidate planning competence by:
- planning for continuity, and progression
- developing a critical perspective *re* curriculum content delivery and organisation whilst recognising and supporting the policy of the school
- demonstrating a working awareness of the contribution own Subject Study can make to the whole primary curriculum

---

TEACHING SKILLS

Work with small groups and on occasion the whole class to:
- gain attention and interest
- sustain involvement
- draw a session to a satisfying close
- explain, demonstrate, instruct
- converse, question, discuss
- praise, check, reinforce, support

then choose organisational strategies to allow for:
- the place of play in learning
- the provision of first-hand experience and learning from real things
- consolidation and practice of basic skills
- an investigative, enquiry-based approach to learning
- a good pace of pupil working

then refine and adapt the above strategies to:
- respond to the learning difficulties or potential of individuals using assessment information
- meet the range of individual needs within the class situation

and develop:
- the ability to challenge bias and negative stereotyping
- the ability to create and sustain a positive classroom ethos

PERSONAL AND PROFESSIONAL DEVELOPMENT

Identify strengths and weaknesses by:
- analysing teaching through discussion
- collaborating with teaching colleagues

then testing out ideas and developing own beliefs about teaching and learning by:
- experimenting with different teaching approaches
- analysing teaching through discussion and theoretical insights
- seeking out and listening to advice and acting upon it

then the development of personal principles and procedures for teaching by:
- sharing views with other people and justifying own teaching in terms of theory and a developing set of values
- recognition of bias, stereotyping and prejudice towards any individual, and seeking to counter it
- initiating ideas

then develop a critical and reflective attitude to the role of the teacher in school and society by:
- maintaining a questioning approach
- holding a responsible attitude to appraisal
- reflecting critically upon the structures and processes of schooling according to how they might advantage/disadvantage individuals and groups
- showing a readiness to accept a leadership role in school

Induction of newly qualified teachers

Your first appointment will be a formative one: the readiness to appraise yourself will be of particular value in what is termed the 'induction' period of your further professional development. The requirement of a period of probationary service for teachers in maintained schools has now been removed, replaced from September 1992 by a period of 'induction'. During this time, as a newly qualified teacher (NQT), you should expect to receive both LEA and school support. In 1992/3 and 1993/4 government funding was made available through the Department for Education's Grants for Education Support and Training programmes. Around forty LEAs were supported in initiating 'induction schemes' in 1992/3, many of which were run in partnership with initial training institutions.

As an NQT entering the profession today, you should, therefore, expect the school in which you work to have an explicit policy and coherent programme for the induction of newly appointed teachers, and be able to seek help and guidance from a nominated member of staff who has been prepared for this role (mentor is the title often used). Self-reflection and analysis will enable you to benefit fully from such a support network.

Schoolteacher appraisal

The induction of NQTs now comes within the framework of professional School-teacher Appraisal schemes ('probationary' teachers were exempt from such schemes when the Schoolteacher Appraisal regulations came into force in 1991). This is another powerful reason for engaging in self-appraisal as a trainee, as self-appraisal, although not compulsory, is a valued component of Schoolteacher Appraisal.

> As part of their preparation for appraisal, schoolteachers should be encouraged to recognise the value of self-appraisal and to carry it out.
> (Calderhead and Lambert (1992) *Induction of Newly Qualified Teachers*)

It plays a significant part in the recognised Teacher Appraisal cycle shown below:

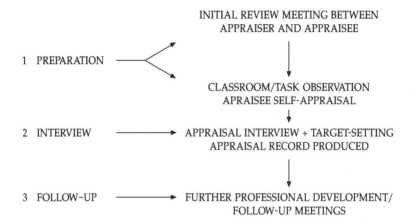

Self-appraisal makes a valuable contribution to each of these stages:

- In the initial meetings, prior reflection upon personal and professional development make it more likely for the discussion to be fruitful.
- Classroom observation can be better targeted if the observer is given a brief to focus upon certain aspects of classroom performance upon which feedback is requested.
- The appraisal interview will be a more balanced affair if the appraisee has appraised his/her own performance, both as classteacher and colleague, before this interview takes place.
- Further professional development is more likely to bear fruit if target-setting and training needs are identified jointly, and relate to self as well as appraiser's perception of need.

Department for education competencies

(as in draft circular 'The Initial Training of Primary Schoolteachers: New Criteria for Course Approval', June 1993)

These include competency in:

- *Curriculum Content, Planning and Assessment,* including ensuring continuity and progression and planning, teaching and testing in the core subjects of the National Curriculum.
- *Assessing and Recording Pupil Progress,* including testing, assessing, giving feedback and reporting on pupil progress.
- *Teaching Strategies,* including awareness of two pupils learning and responding to individual differences; creating and maintaining a purposeful and orderly environment, deploy a range of teaching strategies and select and use resources for learning including IT.

The circular also states under the heading of 'Further Professional Development' that further professional development is anticipated and expected.

Newly qualified teachers should have acquired in initial training the necessary foundation to develop:

- a working knowledge of their contractual, legal, administrative and pastoral responsibilities as teachers
- effective working relationships with professional colleagues
- the ability to recognise the diversity of talent including that of gifted pupils
- the ability to provide for special educational needs and specific learning difficulties
- the ability to evaluate pupils' learning and recognise the effect on that learning of teacher's expectations
- a readiness to promote the spiritual, moral, social and cultural development of pupils
- their professional knowledge, understanding and skill through further professional training
- vision, imagination and critical awareness in educating their pupils

---

SECTION 2: ACTIVITIES

Activity 1: Early reflections

1 At an early stage in your training, complete the Reflection Points shown in the following list.

- What features of primary classroom layout and management interest or intrigue me?

- How do classteachers group children? What reasons do they give? What seem to be the results?
- What do I presently know about how the teachers plan for learning?
- What have I noticed about how teachers gain the attention of children, create interest and enthusiasm, explain things, ask questions, check for learning?

2 After a period of about ten weeks, which should include some time in primary school classrooms, respond to the same questions again.

   Which of your ideas have changed? In what way have they changed? What influenced this change?

3 Answer the following questions at the start of a period of experience in school, and use it to inform your preliminary planning.

- What features of *this* classroom layout and management interest or intrigue me?
- How does *my* classteacher group children? What reasons does he/she give? What seem to be the results?
- What do I presently know about how the teachers in *this* school plan for learning?
- What have I noticed about how *the classteacher* gains the attention of children, creates interest and enthusiasm, explains things, asks questions, checks for learning?

Activity 2: Exploring the dimensions of competence

Using the structure suggested below explore the meaning of the Dimensions of Competence set out in Section 1, pp. 153–5. This is best done in a small group of six to eight people; ideally, the group should include classteachers/mentors, student-teachers and tutors from the training institution.

Suggested structure for the session

1 Working in pairs, think positively about each other's strengths, noting one positive statement about your partner's teaching competence on a strip of card.
2 Share these with the larger group.
3 Working as a group, decide which dimensions each individual's strength would 'fit' under, thus allowing you to come to a better understanding of the profile dimensions.
4 Working in threes and fours, re-write one of the levels of a Dimension of Competence, in a way that you think will be sufficiently 'jargon-free': as to be understandable to a person applying for a teacher-training course.
5 Working in pairs, set targets by each student identifying a target they would like to meet in the coming six weeks.

Creating a profile

1 Create a profile document for yourself, based upon the layout suggested in this chapter.
2 Talk about your strengths and weaknesses with a student-teacher partner.
3 With the help of your partner, write down one positive statement in at least two of the 'evidence' boxes.

Activity 3: Collecting evidence

Here are some suggestions for using *prompt-lists* and *observation schedules* associated with the profile dimensions.

1 Use the prompt list on *Management for Learning* to reflect upon classroom situations in the early stages of your course. It has been designed to help you to reflect upon your 'general classroom awareness'. Choose situations when you are able to act as teacher-helper rather than being directly 'in charge'; this will allow you to think especially about your ability to listen to and talk with children in an appropriate way.

2 Try to answer the questions in the prompt-list on *Teaching Skills* very honestly.

TEACHING SKILLS

In classrooms
- what ways have you used to get the children's interest?
- what things do you do to keep the children involved? Do they always work?
- do you consciously try to alter your voice in some situations? Why? What happens if/when you do?
- are you able to ask questions that let the children tell you what they know?
- can you relax sufficiently to really listen to the answers?
- are the children able to get on with the task when you have finished explaining what to do? If not, can you tell why not?
- do you manage time so that you have time for a concluding talk and for tidying up properly?

In college
- as you learn about teaching methods, do you think about how you might use these?
- do you reflect upon teaching/learning sessions and think about what you might do differently another time?

---

3 Discuss your 'answers' with your mentor.

4 Use your answers and subsequent discussion to determine a focus for a structured observation of one of your lessons.

5 Now that you know what particular teaching skills you wish to have feedback on, turn this prompt-list, and your own list of needs, into an observation schedule, as discussed in the chapter.

MANAGEMENT FOR LEARNING

In classrooms, as you observe
- do you find yourself noticing the layout in relation to how teachers and children move around the space?
- could you list the 'unspoken rules' within one classroom?
- do you know which children are friends?
- can you recognise difference in teacher-talk according to its purpose, e.g. explaining, giving feedback, monitoring behaviour?

In classrooms as you listen, question and teach
- do you spot ways of getting involved?
- how good are you at joining in activities without disturbing, affecting concentration or altering the nature of the activity?
- have you ever re-arranged the classroom furniture for a time?
- can you catch the eye of children, get their attention?
- how do you feel when you are speaking to individuals, a small group, the whole class?
- do you 'hear' your own voice at times? With what effect?
- can you specify 'teacher signals' that work for you?

Activity 4: Lesson evaluation

You will use the *Evaluation* sheet shown in Figure 6.7. Choose a teaching/learning lesson that you have planned *especially* carefully. If possible it should be in an area of the curriculum that you are likely to be teaching again within a few days; otherwise, choose an activity(ies) that you hope to sustain or progress from in subsequent sessions.

1 Evaluate the lesson, using the evaluation format, paying particular attention to the implications section.

2 Plan your next session *in the light* of this evaluation.

3 Evaluate this second session, focusing upon the issues identified first time around. What do you notice?

4 Discuss the two evaluations with your mentor, identifying what has been learned.

Activity 5: Action planning

Using the format shown in the chapter, work out an action plan, on the basis of having completed certain dimensions of the profile after a 'significant' period in your training, e.g. a spell of time in school or a particular unit of your course.

ANNOTATED BIBLIOGRAPHY

Bollington, R., Hopkins, D. and West, M. (1990) *An Introduction to Teacher Appraisal*, Cassell.
  The authors of this text were involved in the project. You will find that:
  • *chapter 1 enables you to see how Schoolteacher Appraisal evolved*
  • *chapter 2 shows how self-appraisal related to the Schoolteacher Appraisal cycle*
  • *chapter 3 outlines strengths and weaknesses of different types of classroom observation.*
Calderhead, J. and Lambert, J. (1992) *The Induction of Newly Appointed Teachers*, General Teaching Council Initiative, NFER.
  You will enjoy this. It will help you to:
  • *see your present initial period of training as a phase within your continuing professional development (pp. 6–7)*
  • *be informed about the induction year as a NQT (pp. 7–17)*
  • *explore some of the issues of profiling (pp. 38–9).*
Dean, J. (1991) *Professional Development in School*, Oxford University Press.
  Two useful chapters to help you see self-appraisal in the wider context of Schoolteacher Appraisal.
Chapter 8, 'Teacher appraisal' gives an overview of:
  • *the development of Teacher Appraisal principles and conditions necessary for effective Teacher Appraisal systems*
  • *Chapter 9, 'Observing Teachers at Work' explores ways of observing in classrooms.*
Dean, J. (1992) *Organising Learning in the Primary Classroom*, Routledge.
  This will help you to reflect on the five profile dimensions we suggest:
  • *chapter 4, 'Teaching Style' will help you to clarify the way in which you prefer to work in classrooms. Although geared to practising teachers, you will find it provokes thought about the sort of teacher you would like to become*
  • *chapter 5, 'The Teacher's Role' provides a set of checklists for analysing a range of teaching skills.*
Delaney, P. (1991) *Primary Staff Appraisal*, Longman.
  A text that enables you to see the issues involved in setting up and relating Teacher Appraisal schemes to whole-school planning and development:
  • *chapter 3 gives a clear overview of the national framework*
  • *chapter 6 deals with classroom observation*
  • *chapter 7, 'The Appraisal Interview' contains material that relates well to giving and receiving feedback more generally.*
Montgomery, D. (1989) *Appraisal in Primary Schools*, Scholastic.
  This book takes a lively and realistic look at Teacher Appraisal. It relates well to many of the aspects of collecting evidence discussed in this chapter:
  • *self-appraisal as the first step to Teacher Appraisal (pp. 23–5)*
  • *chapter 3, 'Classroom Observation' suggests three main categories that observation should fall under and gives lots of advice on observation and feedback techniques.*

Moyles, J. (1988) *Self-evaluation: A Primary Teacher's Guide*, NFER/Nelson.
   This book sets up a model for effective teaching and then uses it as the basis for
   self-evaluation. Compare the criteria suggested here with those of the profile dimensions
   suggested in this chapter.
OFSTED (1993) *Curriculum Organisation and Classroom Practice in Primary Schools: a*
   Follow-up Report, OFSTED.
   See Bibliography, Chapter 4, for commentary.